I0421829

ROE V. WADE
IS UNCONSTITUTIONAL AS JUSTICE BLACKMUN LIED

SUICIDE AND ASSISTED SUICIDE;
CAPITAL PUNISHMENT

BY: DANIEL MCTAGGART

A/K/A Quasi Quasi

Order this book online at www.trafford.com
or email orders@trafford.com

Most Trafford titles are also available at major online book retailers.

© Copyright 2017 Daniel Mctaggart.
All rights reserved. No part of this publication may be reproduced, stored in a retrieval
system, or transmitted, in any form or by any means, electronic, mechanical, photocopying,
recording, or otherwise, without the written prior permission of the author.

Scripture quotations marked KJV are from the Holy Bible, King James Version (Authorized
Version). First published in 1611. Quoted from the KJV Classic Reference Bible, Copyright © 1983.

Scripture quotations marked NASB are taken from the New American
Standard Bible®, Copyright © 1960, 1962, 1963, 1968, 1971, 1972, 1973,
1975, 1977, 1995 by The Lockman Foundation. Used by permission.

Print information available on the last page.

ISBN: 978-1-4907-8210-2 (sc)
ISBN: 978-1-4907-8208-9 (hc)
ISBN: 978-1-4907-8209-6 (e)

Because of the dynamic nature of the Internet, any web addresses or links contained in
this book may have changed since publication and may no longer be valid. The views
expressed in this work are solely those of the author and do not necessarily reflect the
views of the publisher, and the publisher hereby disclaims any responsibility for them.

Any people depicted in stock imagery provided by Thinkstock are models,
and such images are being used for illustrative purposes only.
Certain stock imagery © Thinkstock.

Trafford rev. 06/23/2017

www.trafford.com
North America & international
toll-free: 1 888 232 4444 (USA & Canada)
fax: 812 355 4082

TABLE OF CONTENTS

PREFACE

In 1968 or 1969 I had an interest in joining the Creighton University law review and submitted a 3-page article which showed that one office dictionary definition was that the unborn was a person, a human being. Realizing this, I believe any court would have ruled the status of the unborn was paramount in the constitution, so that the raging abortion controversy could have been stopped early in its tracks.

I was well aware that law reviews didn't print 3-page notes and comments so I was not surprised that the editors chose not to publish the article.

I became Notes Editor my senior year but made no effort to push for publication of my article.

Upon graduation, I became a prosecutor in the Pottawattamie County Attorney's office in Council Bluffs, IA. By late 1972 there had been numerous abortion cases reported with a wide variety of issues discussed, none mentioned the dictionary and its significance. So, I decided to take a hiatus from my prosecutorial position and write the definitive analysis of abortion law.

While doing so, *Roe v. Wade* was announced by the Supreme Court in January 1973. This signaled to me finality and that I should resume my career as attorney. When I examined the case I noted that the court had pared down the number of issues to be considered. Upon close scrutiny, the court's primary opinion seemed to signify that if a pregnant woman wanted to have an abortion it could be called a right of privacy and be granted. This position would collapse if the unborn was a constitutional person.

Its examination of the unborn seemed to be superficial and perfunctory. Its obvious deficiency, as in all the earlier cases, was the omission of the material dictionary definition. Moreover, the lead opinion of Justice Blackmun did not appear to be grounded on sound legal analysis, but amounted to what I call mumbo-jumbo. With such important stakes at hand, the case was a monumental failure.

So, it was my hobby to expose *Wade* as an impassioned biased exercise in futility.

I made three attempts in writing to discredit the case. Each time I realized that my efforts were also futile. My analysis on paper was not convincing to myself.

In January 1974, I was appointed to the judiciary. Still located primarily in Council Bluffs, I had jurisdiction in 9 southwest Iowa counties.

From then until November 1981 I continued with my avocation, probably obsessed, with explaining the folly of *Wade*. At least 9 more attempts were initiated, usually abandoned before completion. My final endeavor exhausted the subject but in my mind, it was only 80% successful, which means I hadn't achieved my goal. It was not fit to be printed.

By late November 1983 I completely considered the case in my mind and realized at this point that I had mastered *Wade* in all respects and that it was a fraud. I was quickly disillusioned with such an incompetent Supreme Court. For this and other reasons I became severely depressed and thought it appropriate to resign as judge, which I did. In that state, I no longer had the presence of mind to write about what I knew or believed. I tossed away all my abortion research.

I concluded I was done with law forever and I turned to religion.

An attorney friend from Omaha, Nebraska asked me to join his firm. I resisted, but reluctantly agreed to work as a law clerk at $6.25 per hour, in February 1984. Eventually, after several hospitalizations, I took on the title of attorney at a raise in pay.

My boss died in 1986 and I remained briefly with his successor.

I'm not sure why, but I decided to tackle the devil *Roe v. Wade* in late 1986. While mistrust for the Supreme Court did, and does continue, I was no longer obsessively depressed.

On the fourth draft I was satisfied in April, 1987, that *Abortion and the Outlaw* was the best pro-life writing produced. Attorney John T. Norman had written *A Private Choice* in the 70's, but I found this book unsatisfactory. In decrying the Court's reliance on privacy, he failed to advance the claim that I found obvious, the availability of the dictionary to solidify the unborn's position, and he offered no strategy to reverse the decision.

Due to lack of funds, *The Outlaw* was not self-published until 1989 when additional notes were added. In retrospect, I blundered on one major point. In Part IV, I summarized and identified 13 major errors in the case, omitting reference to the dictionary even though it was featured prominently in the text.

The book was printed in soft cover, 3 holes punched and 1" fasteners inserted as binding; admittedly the cheapest publication in the history of publishing. To make matters worse, these fasteners didn't work, the pages would fall apart when opened toward the middle. When I learned of this, I experimented with 1 ½" fasteners and the problem was solved. As the books with one inch fasteners were sent to pro-life advocates, they were undoubtedly turned off. I do not hesitate to call this a trashy book about a trashy subject. See chapter 5.

As I considered publication a remarkable achievement and as I would be the sole distributor, I from the outset dated, numbered and signed each book. I believe I'm the only author in the history of the world of publishing to do so.

I printed 2000 books, expecting they would be sold like hotcakes in the pro-life market. I sent copies to many state and national leaders in the movement but got zero feedback. Two publications reviewed the book, one seemed to elevate me amongst some of the world's great thinkers, but I wouldn't have purchased a copy based on these writings.

All in all, I believe I sold 20-25 copies and gave away 200-250. The remainder were discarded. Both reviews have been temporarily misplaced.

When *Planned Parenthood v. Casey* was working its way to the Supreme Court I considered writing an *amicus* brief. I had never done one before, I lived in a small town and there were no typists immediately available. I opted to send *Abortion and the Outlaw* to the Attorney General of the state of Pennsylvania for him to use in his brief.

He never acknowledged the receipt and obviously did not submit anything from it as Justice O'Connor's plurality opinion stated, there was nothing new since *Wade.*

Afterwards, I filed successive lawsuits in Omaha, Lincoln, and Pender, NE and Council Bluffs. Each ended in defeat for different reasons. The last was appealed to the United States Supreme Court but certiorari was denied.

During the course of my litigation, I determined that medical ethics should be given more prominence. I wrote identical 5-page letters to the American Medical Association and all 50 state medical associations and societies raising the question of ethics, which I suggested was their responsibility and not the Supreme Court's. I got no response.

For this reason, plus the fact that I discovered Justice Blackmun actually lied to the Supreme Court in *Wade* and that his lie was perpetuated in subsequent cases, additional notes were warranted. Upon review, I made sure to incorporate the dictionary definition and identified other errors with the total being 30 (possibly 2 were the same so the number might be 29).

In this regard, it might be stated that Professor Tribe of Harvard University also wrote a law review article and book on *Roe v. Wade*. While he was not fully in agreement with Justice Blackmun's rationale, he was satisfied with the result. He did not state that he detected any judicial errors.

Are there 29 major errors in the case or zero errors?

In any event, the initial decision to punch holes and utilize fasteners proved to be a wise one. I am reasonably sure the pro-life leaders were turned off by the book's falling apart with one inch fasteners.

With the addition of the 2001 notes, I can state unreservedly that I am the number one authority on abortion law in the United States.

In the early decade beginning in 2000, I began to write a Bible study guide. It mushroomed into a collection of 43 books which I tentatively entitled *THE THIRD TESTAMENT: an addition to and logical sequel to the Old and New Testaments.* It was my belief that everything that Jesus said was true, but not always recognized at the time. Thus, this would be the first of one or more sources to provide recent evidence of the reliability and truth of his words.

I was hospitalized for a lengthy period. Relatives moved all my belongings out of my apartment, and I am unsure as to whether the text exists. I recall that two or three chapters were unfinished.

In any event, my extensive Bible research led to a passage concerning the acceptability of abortion. I searched Psalms, then Proverbs, then the book of Wisdom to no avail. Finally, in the book of Job I found what I was looking for. It is now clear to me that God is not opposed to abortion, sometimes. A genuine twist in the Old Testament. If there have been 50 million abortions since, January 1973, there are 50 million more souls in heaven.

Roe v. Wade, though based on a fundamental lie, turned out to be consistent with the Bible. *Planned Parenthood v. Casey* chipped into *Wade,* allowing states to make reasonable regulations concerning abortion procedures. As long as they did not commit an undue burden, the Supreme Court is scheduled to take up the issue, in the term beginning October 2015. Many states have responded, with restrictions. These incursions must be carefully examined and fall by the wayside if they are not necessary.

Since, virtually, no one has read, *Abortion and the Outlaw,* this is a repeat and an update, with a new catchy title that should alert pro-lifers and legislators alike. If the matter reaches the judiciary they will be appalled to discover that Justice Blackmun is a devilish liar. He is solely responsible for 50 million abortions. Recognizing *Roe v. Wade* for all these years has paid the highest of dividends.

Today I have convinced myself that this book will resolve the abortion controversy, once and for all. There is no way of telling exactly, but based upon principle I expect the number of abortions, in the United States to decreased from one million per year to less than one thousand-perhaps far less.

My inquiry into abortion in its Biblical context resulted in my examining suicide from a Biblical perspective. It is clear to me, also from the book of Job, that suicide is acceptable to God. This means that physician-assisted suicide is a first amendment right. This matter is important because many people are terminally ill and endure tremendous pain and suffering until they die. If they wish to end the suffering, compassion would dictate that a cessation of suffering, if requested by the patient, is warranted.

In 1997 the United States Supreme Court ruled that a physician did not have a constitutional right to assist in a patient's wish to commit suicide.

The decision was premised on lack of precedent, and the disagreement among a confluence of "experts" from various fields. It is obvious that Job was not considered so it is imperative to revisit the matter immediately. From what I can tell, it is the pro-lifers who are resisting the movement surrounding the process to hasten death requested by a dying patient.

This segment on Capital Punishment was written in the Summer of 2016 with the Nebraska election in mind. Due to circumstances beyond my control, it wasn't printed by Election Day, but the results of the voting were consistent with my conclusions. I would note that the Catholic Bishops tried to influence my vote, but they didn't succeed.

PART I

CONSTITUTIONAL RIGHTS CLASHING

Having temporarily ended the investigation of the constitutionality of abortion laws as held in Roe v. Wade, one is provoked into lashing out at the Supreme Court, considering bombarding them with jars of pickled fetuses. After all, Jane and the unwanted child was nothing short of an almost tearful plea for poor Jane to rid herself of that unwanted child. How does modern woman spell relief for her distress? A-b-o-r-t-i-o-n.

We are tempted to refer to the unborn as an underdog, but that would be a misnomer. In this country, you cannot be cruel to dogs.

Nevertheless, we believe that we have so far discussed the topic in a balanced manner. Our disagreement with *Wade* was unceasing: our continuous harping on *Wade's* shortcomings was justified, we believe. Absent proof to the contrary, we are firmly of the opinion that the unborn in *Wade* was simply not treated fairly. This inequality exists not because we are partisan to the unborn but because procedurally, the unborn was subjected to an injustice simply unknown to American jurisprudence, the right to be heard. In any event we move forward.

DRED SCOTT

Critics of *Wade*[1] have compared the case with the celebrated *Dred Scott* decision.[2] Laying aside issues of procedure and jurisdiction, *Dred Scott* raised the question whether a black man was a citizen of the United States.

The court held that a man of African descent was not and could not be a citizen of the United States.[3] As a non-citizen, Mr. Scott was precluded from suing for his freedom in federal court. The decision also held that the Missouri Compromise was unconstitutional for depriving white persons of the property _ the slaves _ without due process of law.[4]

Similar to *Wade*, *Dred Scott* had the effect of inflaming the nation. Many southerners were delighted; abolitionists and some northerners were very dismayed. A later Supreme Court decision leaves one the impression that it may have contributed to some degree to the Civil War.[5] Scholars debate even until today what the justices actually meant in the decision.[6]

While we find no signs of a civil war over the issue of abortion, we note the charge of immorality being levied against both cases.[7] It is our

---

[1]   See e.g. John T. Noonan, Jr., *A Private Choice* 81-82 (New York: The Free Press 1979).

[2]   Scott v/ Sanford, 19 How 393 (1857).

[3]   *Id.* See also *The Slaughter-House Cases,* 16 Wall. 36 (1872).

[4]   *Scott v. Sandford,* 19 How. 393, 450 (1857).

[5]   *The Slaughter-House Cases,* 16 Wall. 36, 68-73 (1872).

[6]   For one of the most recent discussions, see Don Edward Fehrenbacher, *The Dred Scott Case* (New York: Oxford University Press 1978).

[7]   See footnote 1, supra

States Supreme Court are either consistent with the Constitution or inconsistent with it. It is not really a question of morality. This is not to say that a court should ignore a question of morality, only that considerations of the Constitution should dominate. We may call one that runs counter to the Constitution a bad law, bad in the sense that it is wrong. Lawyers commonly refer to judgments as good or bad decisions.

In our review, we find that, as indicated in the Taney opinion, the blacks had been deemed inferior-one does not ordinarily enslave one's equals or superiors.

view that the opinions of Chief Justice and Justice Daniels bear repeating. First the words of Taney:

They had for more than a century before been regarded as beings of an inferior order, and altogether unfit to associate with the white race, either in social or political relations; and so far inferior, that they had no rights which the white man was bound to respect; and that the negro might justly and lawfully be reduced to slavery for his benefit. He was bought and sold, and treated as an ordinary article of merchandise and traffic, whenever a profit could be made by it. This opinion was at that time fixed and universal in the civilized portion of the white race. It was regarded as an axiom in morals as well as in politics, which no one thought of disputing, or supposed to be open to dispute; and men in every grade and position in society daily and habitually acted upon it in their private pursuits, as well as in matters of public concern, without doubting for a moment the correctness of this opinion.[8]

We can compare the language of Justice Daniel in his concurring opinion: Now the following are truths which a knowledge of the history of the world, and particularly of that of our own country, compels us to know _ that the African negro race never have been acknowledged as belonging to the family of nations; that amongst them there never has been known or recognized by the inhabitants of other countries anything partaking of the character of nationality, or civil or political polity; that this race has been by all the nations of Europe regarded as subjects of capture or purchase; as subjects of commerce or of traffic; and the introduction of that race into every section of this country was not as members of civil or political society, but as slaves, as *property* in the strictest sense of the term.[9]

We note that Taney and Daniel were not necessarily expressing personal views: "This opinion was at that time fixed and universal in the civilized portion of the white race." Taney found a consensus that escaped Blackmun. Daniel touched on the central issue: the negroes came to the

---

[8]   *Scott v. Sandford*, 19 How. 393, 407 (1857).

[9]   *Id.* at 475 (concurring opinion).

colonies and states ·'as slaves, as *property* in the strictest sense". And what is property? The following is the common law view:

> The right of property is that sole and despotic' dominion which one man claims and exercises over the external things of the world, in total exclusion of the right of any other individual in the universe. It consists in the free use, enjoyment, and disposal of all of a person's acquisitions without any control or diminution save only by the laws of the land.[10]

Since the Constitution was silent as to what was property, it was left to the states to define it in any way they wished.[11] As it was deemed advantageous to subjugate those of African descent, laws were enacted to comply. As pointed out in *Dred Scott*, slavery or black property holding was firmly embedded in colonial law.[12]

The constitutional convention struggled with the matter of slavery, and in effect, could not reach a consensus as to what to do at the present time. The great compromise emerged allowing the importation of slaves until 1808,[13] counting three for every five blacks found in a given congressional district;[14] the framers imbued in the Constitution the recognition that the descendants of Africans were unique, were peculiar.

The phenomenal aspect of *Dred Scott* is that none of the justices would acknowledge in the opinion that slavery was wrong. Their analysis ran to more mundane considerations such as the history we have mentioned and the status of freed blacks under state law. But nary a word about the justifiability of slavery as an institution.

That being said, we believe with the Taney majority that the Constitution allowed for the blacks to be treated in a lower class manner as property. The importation clause and the prevalence of slavery at the Constitution's formation sealed their fate. *Dred Scott* was consistent with the Constitution. Any deficiencies should not be attributed to the Taney court but to the Constitution itself. *Dred Scott* was, after all,

---

[10]   William Blackstone I Commentaries. 138

[11]   U.S. Constitution. Amend IX.

[12]   Scott v. Sanford, 19 How. 393. 408-09 (1857).

[13]   U.S. Constitution. Art I. Sec. 9

[14]   Art I Sec 2.

constitutionally sound, we believe, for the Constitution permitted the states to treat the blacks as slaves, as mere property.

The aftermath of *Dred Scott* was a civil war followed by three amendments to the Constitution designed to free the slaves, to make the blacks citizens, to grant them due process rights _ life, liberty and property of their own _ to grant them the protection of equal laws with the whites and to grant them voting rights. Chief Justice Taney had advised that if the Court's decision was unjust, the Constitution should be amended; he proved prophetic. Instead of pointing the finger at the *Dred Scott* court, we should identify the then-existing constitutional framework as the barrier.

What we find curious about *Dred Scott* has already been mentioned, the failure to seize upon the wrongness of making people property. Why didn't the Court discuss that? Why did not the *Wade* court analyze life in the Fourteenth Amendment setting? We would suggest that just as slavery should have been viewed as a clash between liberty and property -- one class of human beings should have the same right of liberty, the same right of property as another _ that abortion should likewise be perceived as a conflict between constitutional life and constitutional liberty. What *Dred Scott* and *Wade* share in common is the failure to explore the issues at its very base. *Wade* was wrong we maintain for failing to explore whether the "life" afforded by Texas to the unborn constituted "life" in the Fourteenth Amendment sense. Regardless of the eventual outcome, the issue begged resolution. Had not Texas given legal life? What else was required for constitutional life? Not a peep from the court. We point to a failure of the courts, *Scott* and *Wade,* to philosophize, to come to grips with the broad form of the Constitution. Had the dissenting justices in *Dred Scott* argued that slavery should not have existed, they would still have been soundly outvoted. The occasion demanded a firm stand against slavery even in a losing effort. Similarly in *Wade:* Does not abortion take life in its Fourteenth Amendment sense? Not even a suggestion of this from the dissenters.

In comparing *Dred Scott* with *Wade,* we recognize that both dealt with controversial subjects - meaning that both praise and condemnation would be forthcoming regardless of the outcome. Both had to make an assessment of history, and we believe the Taney Court fared much better than *Wade.* We have been unable to detect any fundamental error in *Dred Scott,* while *Wade's* historical analysis is suspect time and again. For example, as we have mentioned, all writers on the subject of abortion at common law came to the conclusion that it was a felony at quickening. One writer seemed to suggest otherwise, and *Wade* warmly embraced his suggestion. This writer, Cyril Means, was an outspoken advocate of liberal abortion. The Court and Means were wrong. The *Wade* Court took the view that the purpose of the Nineteenth Century abortion laws was to protect the health of the pregnant woman and not to protect fetal life. James C. Mohr has blown this theory to smithereens by tracking physician after physician who lobbied the various state legislatures to secure protection for the life of the unborn from conception. On this point, the Court was once again pointed into error by Professor Means.

We are not praising *Dred Scott* because we agree with the result, rather because we believe the case was consistent with the Constitution as it then existed. Our criticism is not leveled against *Wade* because of the result reached so much as the manner in which it was reached.

RALEIGH FITKIN

In *Raleigh Fitkin-Paul Morgan Memorial Hospital v. Anderson*, it was ordered by the New Jersey Supreme Court that a pregnant woman undergo a blood transfusion that was deemed necessary to save the child's life and hers.[15] She was refusing the treatment on religious grounds. In this case, there was a battle between the First Amendment liberty of the woman and the right to life of the unborn child. The action was decided at about the ·time the liberal abortion movement was just beginning to ferment. Not a word of criticism was voiced by the legal or medical communities.[16] It was sound law. Life is greater than liberty. The case was cited as authority to the court in *Wade*.[17] The *Wade* court was silent, not mentioning the case.

If religion, a solid first amendment right, is not strong enough to defeat the right to life, explain how privacy, not mentioned in the Constitution, is superior to life. But the Wade Court was silent. Is Raleigh Fitkin right or is Wade? They both cannot be.

---

[15]   201 A2d 537 (1964)

[16]   Note, 33 Fordham L. Rev. 80 (1964)

[17]   35 L. Ed. 2d at 733 (1973).

We believe the newfangled notion of "privacy" caught the justices with their judicial robes unhitched, and in the sensitive and delicate situation, the judges lost their judicial cool, their judicial distance from the affray. First the unborn was not enough of a presence for them to realize that the child was in need of representation; the child's standing was ignored. Then there was one case that was perfect for the unborn's side. *Raleigh Fitkin* stands for the proposition that life is superior to religion or any other form of liberty. If that is right, the pregnant woman's privacy claim amounts to zilch or, in the word of Justice Blackmun, it collapses. How could privacy collapse when the stronghold that could have accomplished the feat was given no opportunity? *Raleigh Fitkin* is a case that cannot be intellectually shunted aside, and it was not in *Wade*. It was ignored just as was the unborn. Taking sides with the pregnant woman who was in distress because she might have a baby, the justices joined the cause of liberation. They forgot to be judges because they forgot the other side. Even the dissenting justices did not perceive that the pregnant woman could cite a thousand cases, and it would not matter, for one little two-page decision out of a New Jersey court system expressed the fundamental principle that befuddled all the justices. In any system governed by the principles of life, liberty and property, if in conflict, life is the dominant value. It is not just happenstance that life is always mentioned first. The Court had never had the opportunity to explain this great concept until *Wade*. And on that historic occasion, it was as if Justice Blackmun and the brethren were marching through the halls of justice chanting: "I went to court, I get to abort,"[18] from the quasi-semi-unofficial theme song of the liberation movement. In one ill-considered moment, the nine cohorts have placed a badge of legitimacy on those who would destroy life. A barrage of abortion was initiated and it has never let up.

Raleigh Fitkin was probably the most significant decision ever presented to the court. Is life more important than liberty? The case escaped the Court's notice or they chose to disregard it.

Earlier we anguished because the Court was not the constitutional philosopher in *Wade*. Is there a philosopher we can turn to? We recall that

---

[18] Reprinted by permission of Quasi Dan Gaius-Daniel.

John Locke wrote about life, liberty and property. We cannot recall any other political philosopher who did likewise. Can he give any assistance?

JOHN LOCKE

In Concerning Civil Government, Second Essay, John Locke declared that "government has no other end but the preservation of property."[19] He defined property somewhat differently than is common today: "his property- that is, his life, liberty, and estate."[20]

For him and everyone else, life comes first. Elsewhere, Locke tells us that "every man has 'property' in his own 'person'. This nobody has any right to but himself. The 'labour' of his body and the 'work' of his hands, we may say, are properly his."[21] The fruits of his labor were his property.

Thus, Locke, who had written by 1690 extolling the virtues of life, liberty and estate, unmistakably said that slavery was wrong:

The natural liberty of man is to be free from any superior power on earth, and not to be under the will or legislative authority of man, but to have only the law of Nature for his rule.[22]

Had this sentiment been observed at the time the colonies became populated, we, of course, would have had no slavery, and perhaps no civil war and perhaps, etc. While we do not intend to dwell on wishful thinking nor list ourselves morally superior to our 17th and 18th Century forebearers, we want to demonstrate that if Locke had been heeded, certain long-range problems would not have developed. Earlier, we gave the opinion that *Dred Scott* was consistent with the Constitution. We can qualify that statement with the utterance that the case disregarded Locke's principles. In any event, Locke followed with his classic definition of liberty:

Freedom, then, is not what Sir Robert Filmer tells us: "A liberty for everyone to do what he lists, to live as he pleases, and not to be tied by any laws"; but freedom of man under government is to have a standing

---

19   John Locke, Concerning Civil Government, Second Essay, VII, 94.
20   Id. at VII, 87.
21   Id. at V, 26.,
22   *Id.* at IV, 21.

rule to live by, common to everyone of that society, and made by the legislative power erected in it. A liberty to follow my own will in all things where that rule prescribes not, not to be subject to the inconstant, uncertain, unknown, arbitrary will of another man, as freedom of nature is to be under no other restraint but the law of Nature.[23]

Under Texas law, the woman would not have the liberty to abort if Locke's definition applied. Since *Wade,* she is at liberty to follow her will. We are also told: "For law, in its true notion, is not so much the limitation as the direction of a free and intelligent agent to his proper interest, and prescribes no farther than is for the general good under that law."[24] We may ask whether the Texas abortion laws were for the general good. There would probably be a difference of opinion.

Children do not have full equality or liberty due to non-age and the lack of reason:

The freedom then of man, and liberty of acting according to his own will, is grounded on his having reason, which is able to instruct him in that law he is to govern himself by, and make him know how far he is left to the freedom of his own will.[25]

The subjection of the minor places in the father a temporary government which terminates with the minority of the child.[26]

Young children are lacking in reason, and we assume no one objects to parental authority as the youngsters are growing.

It is common to associate the concepts of life, liberty and property with John Locke. But the Court has never stated the extent to which the Lockean view has governed the interpretation of the due process clause. From Locke we can identify some minimum standards of life, liberty and property. At a minimum, life should mean the preservation of life and limb. But Locke never define the term further.

At a minimum, liberty should mean freedom under law to do whatever is not prohibited by law. Liberty should not interfere with the preservation of life and limb.

---

23   *Id.*

24   *Id.* at VI, 57.

25   *Id.* at VI, 63.

26   *Id.* at VI, 67.

At a minimum, property in its narrow sense should mean whatever one has acquired with his own hands. At a minimum, it should mean that small children are not at liberty because of their non-age and lack of reason, and are thus subject to their parents and are protected by their parents. Are they protected by their parents prior to birth? Is it too emotional a question? Do not certain physicians recommend a certain diet and a minimum of alcohol and tobacco and the absence of many drugs for pregnant women for the good of the child? Is this wrong? Is this right?

At a minimum, it should mean that no man should claim ownership of a slave. At the time our Constitution was formed and the Fifth Amendment enacted, slavery was a way of life in the southern states, having existed for more than a century and a half. Of course, the framers were quite cognizant of this fact. So when the Fifth Amendment prohibits the deprivation by the federal government of life, liberty and property from any person except by due process of law, by implication, it was clearly intended that a white person should not be deprived of his black property without due process of law, as we have discussed.

We do not mean to say John Locke was the originator of the concepts of life, liberty, property _ for they go back as far as the Magna Charta _ it is to say that he was the only philosopher of note to give meaning to those words, and he was very popular in the American colonies and then states in the Eighteenth Century. [21] The point being when the Court had a very difficult problem involving life and liberty and felt the need to consult philosophers, it is ironic that they overlooked the most significant one of all. Over the years, the Court has had numerous occasions to interpret the due process clause as it relates to property and has dealt extensively with the concept of liberty. There were no occasions when the Court dealt with life _ save the capital punishment cases when the cruel and unusual punishment clause was the focus of attention. Did the Court check all the sources? In a case of first impression of a *possible* person, (like Blackmun's potential life) *possibly* having life under the Fourteenth Amendment in an emotional tug of war, caution and thoroughness should have been bywords. If the Court was going to consult philosophers, why not consult judicial philosophers, those who wrote about jurisprudence or the philosophy of law?

If one examines the Magna Charta, Locke, Blackstone, the Declaration of Independence, and the Fifth and Fourth Amendments,[27] one will find that without exception "life" comes first in the hierarchy of values, as we have already mentioned. It has always been given the highest precedence. According to Blackstone, "[t]he right of personal security consists in a person's legal and uninterrupted enjoyment of his life, his limbs, his body, his health and his reputation."[28] He had life or personal security on top. Also from Blackstone: "Next to personal security, the law of England regards, asserts and preserves the personal liberty of individuals."[29] So not only did the Supreme Court openly reject his view that abortion of a quick fetus was an offense at common law by ignoring the constitutional right of life, the Court implicitly rejected Blackstone's view that life took precedence over liberty. We now cannot place the Wade opinions with the persons and great documents mentioned at the top of this paragraph because Wade neglected to talk about Fourteenth Amendment life. If the liberty and privacy in question are "fundamental", the right to life is obviously the most fundamental of all the rights. For these reasons life should be examined before liberty. If Jane Roe's mother had had an abortion, there would not have been a Jane Roe. This observation is drawn from the examination of "life".

---

27   See Alfred H. Kelly and Winfred A. Harbison, *The American Constitution* 39-40 (New York: Norton & 1963

28   William Blackstone, I *Commentaries* 129.

29   *Id.* at 134.

Locke found abortion to be against God's law; he ranked it with infanticide.[30] Was Locke wrong? While he had a broad definition of liberty,[31] it most definitely did not extend to abortion.

Is the unborn a child? This and the above are all questions that we offer to the Court to discuss freely. The justices in *Wade* did not give serious discussion to these questions. Why? Under the spell of the web that had spread over the country _ the time for liberal abortion had arrived _ it was too emotionally draining for the "liberal" side to ask about whether the act constituted murder. The Court, under the guise of not being biased and emotional aligned itself with the pregnant woman's concern and chose to downplay or to ignore anything that was in conflict.

Consider the following:

There is also the distress, for all concerned, associated with the unwanted child, and there is the problem of bringing a child into a family already unable psychologically, and otherwise to care for it.[32]

Two direct references[33] to the "unborn child."[34] This should signal victory for the unborn child because according to *Webster's Ninth New Collegiate Dictionary,* a child is, in fact, a person: "an unborn or recently

---

[30] John Locke, *Concerning Human Understanding* l, II, 19.

[31] See Mortimer J. Adler, 2 *The Idea of Freedom* 13 (Garden City, N.Y.: Doubleday & Company, Inc. 1961) in his expansive study of liberty placed John Locke with only a few of the philosophers who affirmed four distinct freedoms: (I) the natural freedom of self-determination, (2) acquired freedom of self-perfection, (3) politically beny, (4) circumstantial freedom of self-realization but only as subordinate to and circumscribed by acquired freedom of self-perfection. Thomas Aquinas. Jacques Maritain, Charles Montesquieu and Yves Simon were placed in the same category. The other philosophers who were surveyed affirmed three or less of the freedoms. The only freedom not affirmed by Locke was collective freedom such as is espoused by Karl Marx and Friedrich Engels. *Id.* at 10.

[32] 410 U.S. at 153.

[33] *Id.* 179. (1973).

[34] *Id.* at 184, 190 Cf. *Id.* at 185 in which reference was made to the unborn "child she was carrying."

born person."[35] The dictionary thus indicates that a child is a person." Why didn't the Court reach the same conclusion?

Our examination of the literature reveals that those who favor the "pro-choice" approach to abortion refrain from using the word "child" unless it is modified by "unwanted". Justice Blackmun's employment of the phrase without the modifier makes it appear that he is agreeing that the unborn is a person. When we apply this dictionary concept of person to *Wade*, we conclude a gigantic error occurred in the case. The careful refraining from indicating that the unborn was a person or child in *Wade* was relaxed in *Bolton*.

Consider also the following quotations from John Locke: "[A]ll parents were, by the law of Nature, under an obligation to preserve, nourish and educate the children they had begotten.... "[36] "His command over his children is but temporary, and reaches not their life or property."[37]

Under the Lockean view, the obligation to preserve and nourish extends to a child or children begotten. He did not require a live birth because Locke believed that abortion was a grave wrong.

According to Locke, parents have no "power to make laws, and enforcing them with penalties that may reach estate, liberty, limbs, and life. "[38] He also said:

[Y]et God hath woven into the principles of human nature such a tenderness for their offspring, that there is little fear that parents should use their power with too much rigour; the excess is seldom on the severe side, the strong bias of nature drawing the other way.[39]

Locke did not envision abortion on demand as existing in the United States. He was not privy to the concept of the unwanted child. He would be appalled that life was ignored, that "liberty" or "privacy" had made abortion a fashionable approach to the problem of the unwanted child.

---

[35] By permission. From p. 233 Webster's Ninth New Collegiate Dictionary ©1987 by Merriam-Webster Inc., publisher of the Merriam-Webster'" Dictionaries.

[36] John Locke, *Concerning Civil Government, Second Essay*, VI, 56.

[37] *Id.* at VI, 65.

[38] *Id.* at VI. 69.

[39] *Id.* at VI, 67.

Life, liberty and property are great concepts, great ideas. Life is what the Texas statute provided for the unborn. *Wade* dismissed this as a theory without even bothering to ask whether the Texas view of life was consistent with the Fourteenth Amendment concept of life. We believe that the Court will be forever condemned for failing to raise the inquiry. Locke, on the other hand, is the one to have attempted to explain these great concepts in everyday terms. In his day, there was no systematic assault levied at the magnificent concept of life, so he had no occasion to discuss the meaning of life at length. That historic day came on January 22, 1973, but the entire United States Supreme Court was not paying attention. We would suggest to the Supreme Court that "life" in the Fourteenth Amendment is a theory, and a viable one most places. How does the Fourteenth Amendment theory compare with Texas' theory of life?

CONCLUSION

While we have hopscotched a bit in this part, we believe that we have touched on some important points. In agreeing that slavery is unjust, we have the principles of John Locke to sustain us. But the framers of the federal Constitution did not heed Locke's advice. *Dred Scott* followed ultimately.

Raleigh Fitkin resulted in the right to life of an unborn child having greater value than the child's mother's religion. Life prevails over liberty. Would John Locke approve? Taking into account his disdain of abortion and that "parents were...under an obligation to preserve, nourish...the children they had begotten . . ." we believe we are safe in placing Locke in the "life" category.

In *Wade*, liberty triumphed, but as we have endeavored to show, life was never given a chance. This constitutes one more reason to utter our concern that *Wade* was unfair, that the decision fails to raise the query whether abortion is even compatible with the philosophy of the Fourteenth Amendment. In *Wade*, with the unborn not being a party, no one was present to argue the unborn's case. The case for the unborn rests on the proposition that life is greater than liberty. Instead of holding that liberty is a fundamental right which can be defeated upon a showing of a compelling governmental interest, the hypothesis should have been that life is the most fundamental of all fundamental rights and can be interfered with only rarely. *Raleigh Fitkin* should have alerted the Court to the ascendancy of life over liberty.

In describing the ends of government, John Locke delineated the values of life, liberty and property, a blend of three ingredients, a symmetry, a harmony. He warned that slavery was out of sync with his principles. It took the American colonies and states two centuries and more to eliminate that practice. *Dred Scott* stands as a memorial to the fact that the Constitution as first drawn failed to universalize the three basic rights.

In the Twentieth Century, *Raleigh Fitkin* stood before the Court as a beacon, a reminder that life is greater than liberty. Gazing through eyes that could only have been inspired by the women's liberation movement, the Court did not see little *Raleigh Fitkin,* or if it did, its eyes were shielded by blinders as the Court forged ahead shaking the Lockean principles to their very foundation. Tossing the loaded dice up turned liberty for the majority. The great preservers of the Constitution, unmindful apparently of their remarkable achievement, retired from the constitutional plane, unaware that *Roe v. Wade* had done the unthinkable in elevating liberty to a higher constitutional perch than life. Another error was wrought on the unborn.

In placing life at the top, we are necessarily placing liberty on a lower rung; they are not co-equals. Does liberty mean today what it meant when the Fourteenth Amendment was drafted? Has the meaning of life changed?

We can find no case in which liberty was described or defined in the Fifth Amendment prior to 1868. With the Constitution providing no definition, we will return to William Blackstone who tells us:

This personal liberty consists in the power of locomotion, of changing situation, or removing one's person to whatsoever place one's own inclinations may direct; without imprisonment or restraint unless by due course of law.

Compare this with the three-prong description provided by Justice Douglas in *Wade:*

First is the autonomous control over the development and expression of one's intellect, interests, tastes, and personality.[40] Second is freedom of choice in the basic decisions of one's life respecting marriage, divorce, procreation, contraception, and the education and upbringing of children.[41]

Third is the freedom to care for one's health and person, freedom from bodily restraint or compulsion, freedom to walk, stroll or loaf.[42]

Even though a majority has not joined in, we cannot state that Douglas spoke incorrectly. The history of liberty in the Fourteenth Amendment during the Twentieth Century has been one where in numerous cases the Court has pinpointed these various aspects of liberty, specifying the extent to which these forms of liberty are protected from state encroachment. It has invariably been a balancing test, the individual liberty claim versus the government's attempt at regulation or control.

It seems clear, even from a cursory glance, that liberty has come a long way_ it has broadened so much _ since the time of Blackstone.

Life has been, or so it seems, a neglected feature of the Fourteenth Amendment. Perhaps neglected is inappropriate; further reflection leads us to believe that life has been such an overarching force, that the states have done admirably well in not depriving persons of life without due process. We would suggest that if the state government does a fine job of protecting life, there will be few cases in court raising life due process violations. Turning to the issue of abortion, we can realize that since the enactment of the Fourteenth Amendment in 1868 and the mid-1960's, all states protected the life of the unborn. When the states protected the life so adequately, there existed no reason to go to court seeking further protection for the unborn. Thus in 1973 the unborn truly came before the court as a stranger. A rude awakening was waiting.

Let us turn the tables a bit in *Wade*. Let us assume that the Court had focused on the unborn before becoming entangled in privacy. Our imaginary conclusion: "We hold that the unborn had life under Texas law and the unborn having been found by the Texas legislature to constitute human life, we believe the requirement has been met to denominate this

---

[40]   William Blackstone, I *Commentaries* 130.

[41]   410 U.S. at 211. (Emphasis removed.)

[42]   *Id*. (Emphasis removed.)

as life within the Fourteenth Amendment... we find that the unborn is a Fourteenth Amendment person . . . we will now turn to the woman's claimed right of privacy ...".

Under this type of holding, the arguments of Justice Blackmun are pitifully meagre. This life causes you distress? You do not want the child? You do not want the stigma of unwed motherhood? In a fair fight, life will beat out liberty every time because life is stronger, more basic and more important.

To the Supreme Court: there is something the unborn has been meaning to tell you since 1973...

Back to reality. In late June, 1972, a majority of the Supreme Court in the capital punishment cases extended life to several hundred felons convicted of heinous offenses.[43] Less than seven months later the unborn, whose only offense was to exist, was before the Court: "Brother, can you spare a life _ or several million." The Court was stone-deaf, not bothering to discuss life in its constitutional setting, brushing aside the unborn as some form of nebulous *potential/life*.

Roe v. Wade gives new meaning to the Shakespearean words: "To be or not to be, that is the question." While giving lip service to the fact that the unborn was an embryo and then a fetus, the Court never did come to grips with the reality that the unborn is a being, separate and distinct from the pregnant woman. This may account for why the unborn was snubbed so by the Court.

The lack of participation in the case by the unborn, the failure to raise and discuss basic issues on behalf of the unborn, the bias, the failure to discuss life in its constitutional setting, when taken together, provide sobering evidence that the Supreme Court never took the unborn seriously. This explains why the challenge between life and liberty fizzled out without ever getting off the ground.

---

[43] *Furman v. Georgia*, 408 U.S. 238 (1972).

PART II

PROVING THE UNBORN'S CLAIM

ISSUES AND THE FOURTEENTH AMENDMENT PERSON

Insofar as the unborn is concerned, the following are basic issues.

1. *Whether the unborn constitutes life under state law.* We recognize that Texas so defined the unborn, but the Supreme Court rejected this "theory of life."
2. *Whether the unborn constitutes life within the meaning of the Fourteenth Amendment.* The Court did not discuss whether the Fourteenth Amendment had a "theory of life" as a base.
3. *Whether the unborn is a person under state law. Wade* held that the unborn is not a person in the whole sense.
4. *Whether the unborn is a person within the meaning of the Fourteenth Amendment.*

Without defining the Fourteenth Amendment person, the Court rebuffed the unborn.

In its treatment in *Wade*, the Court focused on the Fourteenth Amendment person and viewed the issue of personhood from several perspectives which may be summarized as follows:

1. No case could be cited that held a fetus was a person within the meaning of the Fourteenth Amendment.[1]

---

[1]   410 U.S. at 157.

18

2. The Constitution does not define "person." In many places where the word is used in the Constitution, it can apply only postnatally.[2]

3. As was stated earlier by the Court: abortion practices were freer during the Nineteenth Century than today.[3]

4. The Court's prior decision in *United States v. Vuitch* would infer the same effect "for we there would not have indulged in statutory interpretation favorable to abortion in specified circumstances if the necessary con sequence was the terminating of life entitled to Fourteenth Amendment protection."[4] *Vuitch* held that the wording of a restrictive abortion law, allowing an abortion when necessary to protect a woman's health, was not vague.

We can examine the Court's reasons for excluding the unborn point by point.

First, if no case could be cited holding the unborn to be a person in the Constitution, neither could a case of the U.S. Supreme Court be cited to show that the unborn was *not* such a person in 1973. It was an open issue, a question of first impression. After all, it was not until 1969 that the Supreme Court held a minor child to be a Fourteenth Amendment person[5] until the time that a corporation was held to be a Fourteenth Amendment person in 1886, the same could have been said about it.[6] Not until the late 1960's did there exist a factual basis to claim that the unborn was not a person, making it necessary to raise the issue for the first time. Thus, when an issue is raised for the first time, it obviously cannot have been decided before.

Second, it bears repeating that most of the time the word "person" is used in the Constitution, it cannot apply to the corporation.[7] Yet, the corporation enjoys Fourteenth Amendment status. We are not concerned

---

2   *Id.*

3   410 U.S. at 158.

4   410 U.S. at 159.

5   *Tinker v. Des Moines*, 393 U.S. 503, 511 (1969).

6   *Santa Clara County v. Southern Pacific RR*, 118 U.S. 394 (1886).

7   See 410 U.S. at 157. See text at note 60 Part I *supra*.

with any provision other than the Fourteenth Amendment. The first question should have been: *Can* the unborn be a Fourteenth Amendment person?

In noting that the Constitution did not define person, Justice Blackmun apparently saw no need for the Court to do so either. How can we really know whether the unborn is a Fourteenth Amendment person unless we first know what a Fourteenth Amendment person is? This question should be a continuing thorn to the Court until a resolution is offered. Third, we believe it was shown previously that abortion practices were free for perhaps four decades during the Nineteenth Century. It was this freedom that prompted reaction from the physicians, who believed abortion to be a moral wrong.[8] Responsible physicians could not ethically perform abortions, did preach about the evils of abortion and did secure passage of stricter laws. The key consideration is the Fourteenth Amendment. Did not abortion laws become more restricted at about the time it was adopted and within the next two decades?

Fourth, in *United States v. Vuitch,*[9] the Court specifically reserved ruling on the constitutionality of abortion statutes.[10] It is simply unfair later to declare otherwise. Finding the Court's analysis of the Fourteenth Amendment person deficient for failing to identify or define the person, we will search out our own meaning for the word.

AN EXAMINATION OF THE "EXPERTS"

A human being or not a human being? A rather simple question, or is it? If Justice Blackmun could have found a consensus among the doctors, philosophers and theologians, he implied quite strongly that the unborn would be a Fourteenth Amendment person. What would these professionals do if they were asked to give an answer as to whether the corporation were a human being or a Fourteenth Amendment person? We think they would reach unanimity that the corporation was not a

---

[8] James C. Mohr, *Abortion in America* 166.

[9] 402 u.s. 62 (1971).

[10] *Id.* at 71-72. "Since that question of vagueness was the only issue passed upon by the District Court, it is the only issue we reach here." *Id.* at 73. (Citations omitted.)

human being, and they would probably say that the matter of Fourteenth Amendment persons is better left to someone else. But that someone else, nine judicial officers, declared they could not decide on the unborn because the doctors, philosophers and theologians could not agree. Has the Supreme Court delegated certain of its responsibilities to some unnamed indefinite professionals?

In reading the text of *Roe v.Wade,* we find that the word "human being" is not used once. This is somewhat curious because the view that the unborn was human seemed to be put forth with much vigor by the right to life proponents. These amici curiae, in outlining "at length and in detail the well-known facts of fetal development,"[11] attempted to demonstrate that the unborn was a human being and therefore a Fourteenth Amendment person.

In rejecting these assertions, the Court was more impressed with the fact that philosophers, theologians and physicians all disagreed among themselves. Since these "experts" were hopelessly in conflict, the Court was unable to reach a direct conclusion" at this point in the development of man's knowledge."[12] Hence, the Court's acceptance of the nebulous terms "potential life"[13] or "potentiality of human life."[14] We are dismayed at the Court's employment of' 'potential life." What is the difference between this and actual life? How do we know that this is not Fourteenth Amendment life? Please, Justice Blackmun, define the terms "potential life" and Fourteenth Amendment person.

It may be for good reason that the Court did not use the words human being. Were they afraid to use the term? Or did not it make a difference? With us sitting here pen in hand, we can write at some length and still not know what went into their judicial thinking. We raise the question as to how one can write for pages on abortion and not once mention the main claim of the unborn: I am a human being.

Should we listen to the claims of the unborn to be recognized as a person, as a human being? Don't we have to rely on the doctors, philosophers and theologians?

---

[11]   410 U.S. at 156.

[12]   *Id.* at 159.

[13]   *Id.* at 150.

[14]   *Id.* at 162.

We have read several dictionaries that defined "person" as a human being. None of them added the qualification of having to be so recognized by the big three. So the fact that it is commonly believed by a number of people that the unborn does qualify as a human life from day one mean anything at all? We recall that the physicians of the Nineteenth Century were firmly of that belief. Note carefully that their Twentieth Century successors did not go on the record as declaring those beliefs from the previous century as being wrong. Rather, the AMA said it would follow state law. The time has long since passed when someone should take literally the modern medical profession and shake its members by the collar and demand an answer: is the unborn a human being under any medical definition?

What of the theologians? We are simply at a loss for words as to why the Court would focus on theologians. First of all, which theologians do you choose? Second and more important, it seems to reek of encroachment on the First Amendment's separation of Church and State. The unborn would ask the Supreme Court to disinvite all members of the clergy when the unborn's status next comes under review.

And the philosophers? In reading the *Wade* opinion, one gets the impression that philosophers living before Christ get votes witness the sighting of the Stoics in *Wade*.[15]

As it is too late to try and persuade the Stoics, we have no way of ever arriving at consensus. Moreover where the Court the next time to give credence to philosophers, the unborn would request that each of the philosophers be named and otherwise identified. Can we look to a philosopher of another nation? Can the unborn have the right to cross-examine these philosophers to perhaps pinpoint that there are numerous fundamental questions that the philosophers disagree among themselves. So that disagreement about abortion might not only be predictable but inevitable. The Court spoke of those "trained in philosophy." Many have received some training in philosophy but might not consider themselves qualified as a philosopher. Additionally, philosophers are not licensed by state law. In what other instance has the Court declared as a matter of constitutional law that it was first a matter of finding the consensus of

---

[15]   See 410 U.S. at 160.

these three groups? We are tentatively wondering whether we can dismiss the theologians and philosophers.

Philosophers over the years have struggled in an attempt to isolate the essence of man. To the present day, there is no satisfactory definition of human being. As stated by John Locke:

And I imagine none of the definitions of the word *man* which we yet have, nor descriptions of that sort of animal, are so perfect and exact as to satisfy a considerate inquisitive person; much less to obtain a general consent, and to be that which men would everywhere stick by....[16]

Thus, if we consider that we cannot agree on the essential characteristics of any adult human being, it should also follow that we would not agree if and when an unborn child has acquired the necessary characteristics to be called a human being. At present there appears little likelihood of philosophers, theologians and medical scientists reaching a consensus on the issue. Perhaps had the *Wade* court recognized that the three groups would not have reached a consensus on the adult human being, it would have recognized the shortcomings of expecting agreement on the issue of the unborn. To the Supreme Court: If the theologians, philosophers and physicians cannot agree on why the ordinary adult is a human being, does it not seem to be a mistake _ no an absurdity_ to expect agreement on the unborn's status as a human being? The presence of philosophers and theologians does little but cause confusion.

VEGETABLE, ANIMAL OR HUMAN

The unborn expects to have to contend with the men and women of medical science. If the unborn is to exist as a person it must be because of recognition by the physicians. But please do not sic the clergy and the philosopher-types on the unborn's case. Do not ask the unborn to contend with every single one of them.

---

[16]   John Locke, *Concerning Human Understanding* III, VI,

The unborn's favorite definition of "person," found in some dictionaries, is a human being as contrasted with an animal or thing.[17] We call this a three-choice definition.

Philosophers, or so we think, like to hem-haw about whether sufficient development has occurred to pronounce the unborn a human being. The beauty of this particular definition - which we did not see addressed in *Wade* in any fashion - is that it eliminates much debate, it provides only three choices.

Many centuries ago, Aristotle wrote that the unborn began life as a vegetable, transposed into an animal, and finally became a human being prior to birth.[18] No one before Aristotle had set forth this theory. It will be remembered that Aristotle was both a philosopher and a scientist. As a scientist, he was putting forth his thesis that successive stages led from the nutritive or vegetable soul to the sensitive or animal soul and finally the human or rational soul. Thomas Aquinas, the philosopher-theologian, took these scientific principles as his own, adopting similar conclusions as

---

[17]   *Random House Dictionary* 1074 (1967): *person:* "2. a human being as distinguished from an animal or a thing.·· See also 7 *The Oxford Dictionary* 724; *Webster's Seventh New Collegiate Dictionary* 630.

[18]   See Eugene Quay, "Justifiable Abortion- Medical and Legal Foundations," 49 Georgetown L.J. 395, 427 quoting from Aristotle, *De Generatione Animalium*, ii, iii, col. 736a, line 28-col. 736b, line 9 (Platt trans!. 1910). See also: John F. Donceel, S.J., "Immediate Animation and Delayed Hominization," 31 *Theological Studies* 76, 76-77: "The question of the status of the embryo seems to have come up for the first time in the works of Aristotle. In his *On the Generation of Animals*, Book 2, Chaps. 1-4, Aristotle says that the embryos of animals and of man are first animated by a vegetative or nutritive soul, which is followed by a sensitive or animal soul when the embryo i s sufficiently organized to receive it. In the case of man, this animal soul itself is succeeded by a rational or human soul whose origin is difficult to explain," citing Aristotle, *On the Generation of Animals* 735a 15-26; 736a 35-736b 16 (tr. A.D. Beck [London, 1953] pp. 192 ff.).

Aristotle.[19] But according to our ground rules of bypassing philosophers and theologians, we can retain Aristotle the scientist and ignore Aquinas the philosopher-theologian.

The problem with Aristotle is that this thesis has been relegated to mystery and history. It is no longer seriously believed that the three-part change from vegetable to animal to human has validity.[20] In Twentieth Century thinking, this is stated in terms of human being, not a vegetable and animal. In the end, Aristotle was correct in labeling the unborn as a living being, which scientifically can be only the vegetative, animal or human life. Where he was incorrect was in proposing that the human unborn went through these stages of development. On this point, modern scientists can declare Aristotle wrong and reject his proposition. Our three-choice definition adheres to the generally accepted position that Aristotle was in error with regard to the human stages of development, while his theory that all living beings had to be plant (or vegetable), animal or human remains valid scientifically speaking.[21]

Here is where the well-known facts of fetal development would come into play. For one could take any point of fetal growth and state what

---

[19] Joseph F. Donceel, S.J., "Immediate Animation and Delayed Hominization," 31 *Theological Studies* 76, But see former Justice Tom C. Clark, "Religion, Morality and Abortion: A Constitutional Appraisal ", 2 Loyola (L.A.) L. Rev. 1, 5 (1969): "Some physicians argue that abortion should be permitted with impunity at any time up to the sixth month of pregnancy since prior to that' time the fetus is no more than a growing plant," citing Stern,.. The Issue of Legalized Abortion," 88 Can. Med. Ass'n. J. 899 (1963); J. Fletcher, *Morals and Medicine* 152 (1967); address by E. Bradenton, Symposium of Christian Medical Society, Aug., 1968.

[20] Steven Jay Gould, *The Panda's Thumb*, (New York: W.W. Nonon & Company 1980) 222, states that it is generally accepted that there are five kingdoms: plants, animals, fungi, protists and prokaryotes monerans. We suppose in this estimation humans are part of the animal kingdom. We would suggest that since physicians treat humans and veterinarians generally limit their services to all other animals but man, that humankind is yet a separate kingdom. Rest assured man does not fall into the categories of fungi, protists and prokaryotes monerans, as is. explained by Gould.

[21] See text at note 17 Supra.

evidence indicated a human being, what evidence indicated an animal and what indicated a vegetative thing. Clearly, with the disavowal of Aristotle's view of three-stage transition, we believe, it is no longer reasonable to call the unborn a vegetable or animal at any time. But much of the dispute surrounding the unborn may revolve on this point. Thus, we find that the biology texts used in high school and college provide support for this contention. We have yet to find a biology book which includes the human unborn in the section on plants or animals. Additionally, we have three distinct scientists who deal with the plant, animal and human: the botanist and horticulturalist, the veterinarian, and the physician, respectively.

If one does choose to call the unborn a vegetable or animal, the inquiry is not finished. Which vegetable? Which animal?

Should this three-choice definition be used? If not, why not? The definition has existed for many years. It was not created with the abortion dilemma in mind.

Many might be ready to applaud the Court's statement that when those trained in philosophy, theology and medicine are unable to reach a consensus, the Supreme Court is unable to speculate as to the answer. Why must there be unanimity among the groups? As has already been noted, *no one* has been able to capture the real essence of adult human beings. [23] Second, the Court has never before searched for such a consensus before deciding what is a Fourteenth Amendment person.[22] Third, the three-choice definition does not invoke these elitist experts, with the possible exception physicians or other scientists.

ROLE OF PHYSICIANS

The three-choice definition, if utilized, provides one more reason that we can do away with the pesky philosophers and theologians who cannot come to an agreement.

The physicians are an entirely different matter. They are scientists. By education, training and experience, they deal every day with the care

---

[22] *Levy v. Louisiana,* 391 U.S. 68, 70 (1968) (illegitimates); *Santa Clara County v. Southern Pacific RR.,*118 U.S. 394 (1886) (corporation); *Yick Wo v. Hopkins,* 118 U.S. 356 (1886) (aliens).

and treatment of human beings, including the unborn. The American Medical Association must be told: Put away all extraneous considerations _ especially as to philosophy and theology and that which might be emotional underpinnings _ and determine to the best of your ability whether the unborn of the human is a human being, an animal or a vegetable. Is it not agreed that the unborn is a living being? If so, what kind? "That abortion is an act which kills something - a being of *some* sort - is not in dispute; that is the purpose of abortion techniques."[23]

Questions premised on the kind of being should have been raised and answered definitely in 1970 by the AMA. It might be well to consider two hypothetical physicians who deal with the unborn. To physician goes a pregnant woman who wants an abortion because she does not want her pregnancy or the unborn child. Physician A listens to her and then tells her his views. He states that from his perspective, she is carrying a human child and abortion would thus be very wrong. He offers prenatal treatment. She leaves his office and goes to Physician B who hears the same story, sets up an appointment for the abortion and carries out the patient's wishes.

Admittedly, the above is a very skimpy scenario, but it is intended to dramatize a very important point: either Physician A or Physician B is acting unethically. Physicians have the solemn responsibility to treat and heal all human beings under their care. If Physician B is correct, then Physician A is in the wrong, and vice-versa. Assuming that the woman is eight weeks pregnant, one would expect that the medical profession should tell all the doctors whether this constitutes a human being, an animal or a vegetable at that stage of gestation or for that matter, at any point in development. Science offers no other choices. The eight-week-old child cannot be a human being in Physician's office and a nondescript object at Physician B's. Someone- the AMA - must recognize how utterly moronic it is to pretend that either or both A's and B's office practices are perfectly acceptable. We would invite the reader to consult with his

---

23   Daniel Callahan, *Abortion, Law, Choice and Morality* 377 continues: "Or if the word 'kills' seems too strong, and we want to speak more euphemistically, one can at Least say that induced abortion is an act which stops a specifiable development process: the development of the product of conception, the conceptus."

or her own physician about the three choice definitions. Given that the definition is in the dictionary and appears to apply to the unborn, inquiry with a physician would seem to be appropriate. "Doctor, would you agree that science classifies all living beings as human, animal or vegetable?" "Doctor, would you say that at conception the unborn is a human being, an animal or a vegetable?" If the physician states either of the latter two, ask which vegetable or which animal. Question whether any scientific treatises recognize the human unborn with plants or animals. If so, describe the kinds of plants and animals with which the unborn is identified. If one were going to have a lengthy conversation, one might even ask the physician for the view, of known, of the American Medical Association. Has the AMA considered the unborn from the vegetable-animal-human perspective?.

The American Medical Association of more than a century ago acted in a certain manner because it was convinced that the unborn constituted human life from conception.[24] The American Medical Association of today has voted to go along with state law, whatever that may happen to be In 1973, the Supreme Court made it easy by requiring the states to allow abortion on demand as long as the pregnant woman can find a physician willing to perform the service.[25]

The American Medical Association has gotten off easy because it has not been compelled to answer the same question propounded by the AMA in the last century: Is this human life? If the AMA concludes that a pregnancy of eight weeks or whatever duration does not constitute a live human being, it should direct to all members not to medically treat *that* (animal, vegetable or whatever) until such time as *that* becomes a human being. Physician A should treat human beings only. Aye, there's the rub. The AMA of yesterday did not take the cushy approach to abortion. Its members literally marched to the state capitols and demanded that a wrong be righted.[26] The AMA of today does not know whether abortion is right or wrong. Rather, it lets the state decide.

---

[24] 410 U.S. at 142. See also James C. Mohr, *Abortion in America* 200-.

[25] 410 U. S. at 143.

[26] James C. Mohr,. Abortion in America 157.

Assume for a moment that the AMA were to re-examine the point raised above and were to conclude that the unborn is a human being. How would the AMA tell its members that they must comply with the new approach and thus refuse to cooperate with the Supreme Court? For the *Wade* decision does depend upon a willing group of physicians. If all physicians were unwilling to or ethically prohibited from performing abortions, the effect of *Wade* would be nullified, with no one left to carry out the request to abort. Perhaps this colored the thinking of Justice Blackmun when he wrote about the Hippocratic Oath.[27]

More than likely in such case there would be some who wanted to carry on the abortion business, and there would be an open conflict between medical ethics and the physician's obligation to see that constitutional rights _ ala *Wade* _ are being met. Asking the general question "is this a human being?" invites endless argument when the unborn of the human is scrutinized. This is what confronted the *Wade* Court. Substitution of the three-choice definition, however, pointedly allows for but three possibilities. Under this definition, one does not search out the philosophers or theologians. One asks the blunt question: which is it? The physicians could be helpful. So far, they have not been. From leaders in one epoch to followers at a later time. Should we not ask the physicians to assume leadership roles? Do not they belong in the forefront?

Is our Wisconsin person a human being because it would have been absurd to call it an animal or vegetable or other thing?

The three-choice definition may be tough for the squeamish, but if one calls the unborn of the human a vegetable, the follow-up question is which vegetable? Similarly, if one chooses animal, one must be prepared to state which animal and have available facts to support the choice.

The Wisconsin human being, we have seen, was defined as a human being from the moment of conception. This is a theory of life that neither Texas, Wisconsin nor any other state may adopt under *Wade*. Despite the presence of the three-choice definition, state are not allowed to call the

---

27   See 410 U.S. at 130-32. The result would inevitably be a clash between medical ethics and the Constitu tion: the physician wanting to perform an abortion would claim that medical ethics would violate the constitutional right to perform an abortion.

unborn a human being. Instead of human being, shall we call the unborn an animal or other thing to satisfy the Court? The fact of the matter is that the Supreme Court's use of raw judicial power does not comport with the dictionary. Must the meaning in the dictionary be changed to comply with the Court's pronouncement?

Ask a veterinarian about a pregnant cow, dog, cat or other animal. He will tell you in a flash that the cow is carrying a calf, that the dog is carrying puppies and the cat, kittens. This is common knowledge among all who have the use of reason. Is there any stage where the kittens are not part of the cat family? All of the above are babies of their own species. One wishes to invite the philosophers, theologians and medical scientists to do research and come up with a view on the status of the cat's litter, one week in development. Would they figure out that those were kittens from the earliest moments? In *Levy v. Louisiana, the* Supreme Court stated:

We start from the premise that illegitimate children are not "non persons." They are humans, live, and have their being. They are clearly "persons" within the meaning of the Equal Protection Clause of the Fourteenth Amendment.[28]

The same statement fits the unborn of the human race whether wanted or unwanted: they are (1) humans because they are not animals or other things; (2) live, since if they were not there would be a miscarriage; and (3) have their being which is not disputed. It is not contested that the unborn is a being separate from his/ her mother, though dependent on her. With the three-choice definition of person coupled with the above passage, there is a proof that the unborn belongs in the Fourteenth Amendment. Perhaps we can uncomplicated the abortion puzzle by eliminating considerations of "population growth, pollution, poverty and racial overtones," as suggested in *Wade*, by minimizing the effect of philosophers and theologians, by ascertaining and embracing what is legitimately contained in the dictionary and what is scientific.

We would suggest that the burden should rest with the opponents of the unborn to demonstrate that the three-choice definition is not a valid argument on constitutionality, both because it is a dictionary or settled definition, and it does comport with modern science.

---

[28]   *Levy v. Louisiana,* 391 U.S. 68 (1968).

THE INFERIOR HUMAN BEING

What or who is an inferior human being? Our first thought is that in our nation we are all considered equals. Perhaps the concept of inferior human beings belongs to antiquity. It can be remembered that Chief Justice Taney so characterized the black race in *Dred Scott.*[29] While it certainly is not pleasurable to recall the decision in this respect, it was an accurate statement at the time. By and large, the white society that employed and tolerated black slavery considered the blacks to be inferior. We cannot eradicate history today by wishing it were not so.

It is submitted that today's inferior human beings are the unwanted, unloved unborn. We have a name for those unborn children who are wanted, we shall call them david, with a small d. Correspondingly, we shall refer to the unwanted as undavid. Every thinking human being who is alive today can recognize that when he/she was in the womb, an abortion would have resulted in the termination of life or the death of that being. All of us are alive today either because we were wanted by our parents or because abortion was illegal or both. This holds true for the nine justices who decided *Wade* by a 7-2 vote. The unborn children who are wanted are consequently the superior children because they are given the opportunity to continue to develop, to continue to experience life. The roughly twenty-one million unborn children whose lives have been snuffed out by abortion since *Wade* are modem society's inferior human beings. david is of value to his parents, undavid is not. Whereas the law used to provide protection for all undavids, *Wade* has wiped that out.

When the three-choice definition and the inferior human being are taken together, the observations set forth above seem to logically follow. When the unborn in Wisconsin are considered as human beings from conception, all of the state's unborn are fully, equal human beings possessing the right to live, the only right needed for survival. There were no legally inferior human beings in Wisconsin until the *Wade* decision. Then there became two classes. Today's inferior human beings are subjected to a fate worse than slavery. It is called death. Today's inferior human beings are aborted and discarded like trash. Unwanted, inferior,

---

[29]   19 How. 393, 407 (1857).

good riddance. In the *Wade-feminist view*, one does not mention death as having any bearing on the abortion process.

When one is seeking to abolish the concept of inferior human being, one is seeking equal protection of life for all human beings. It is curious that Blackmun did not visualize that the abortion ethic creates the two classes of being: david's, those destined to live and undavids, those destined to die. While the combination of philosophers, theologians and physicians might have confused Justice Blackmun on the issue of humanity, nobody, we believe, caused confusion on the fact that abortion ends in a dead being _ an inferior dead being. Perhaps the Court did not deem this significant.

THE LEGAL PERSON

Legal person is defmed as: "a human being (natural person) or a group of human beings, a corporation, a partnership, an estate, or other legal entity (artificial person or juristic person) recognized by the law as the subject of rights and duties."[30]

This definition of person opens the floodgates so that many entities other than human beings can be included. The corporation, for example, is often called an "artificial person" because it is not a normal human being.

The unborn claims legal personality either because it is a human being or because it is one of those "other legal entities". The state may give legal rights to an animal or thing. You will note that Justice Douglas urged that a valley, and alpine, meadows and rivers be made legal persons.[31] The key consideration is that the entities have legal rights. If I have legal rights, then I necessarily am a person.

The right to life is, of course, a legal right. The Wisconsin human being that has been referred to from time to time is a superior example of the unborn being called a human being and being given the right to live by the duly elected Wisconsin lawmakers. The Texas law was similar; it was the "life of the fetus or embryo." In other words, the State of Texas gave to the unborn the legal right to life: a real and true legal right. With

---

[30]   Random House Dictionary 1075 (1967).

[31]   Sierra Club v. Morton, 405 U.S. 727 (1972).

the right to life, other fundamental rights are irrelevant to the unborn's status. The unborn does not need the right to vote, religion or speech - perhaps someone else can speak for the unborn.

Other states a century ago similarly bestowed the right to life on the unborn child. They did not all do so in terms as explicit as Wisconsin's and Texas', but it is clear from the lobbying efforts done by medical societies that this is what occurred.[32] A statute need not read: an unborn child has the right to life. It is enough that abortions are forbidden from conception. From that point on the right to life exists. The Nineteenth Century laws commonly accorded the right to live except in cases where necessary to protect a woman's life. At common law, abortions were made illegal from quickening. When the protection later was extended to conception, the right to life existed from conception.

What is dismaying is that the majority of the *Wade* justices did not perceive this important point.

In property law, the right of the unborn to inherit property has existed for more than two centuries and is present in virtually all the states:

It has been the uniform and unvarying decision of all common law courts in respect of estate matters for at least the past 200 years that a child en ventre sa mere is "born" and "alive" for purposes of his benefit.[33]

To inherit property is certainly to his benefit _ a legal right conferred, making the unborn a legal person. This legal right to inherit must be respected by all. Any interference with this right could and would result in legal action. The unborn child is on equal footing with the born child and the adult for inheritance purposes. Regarding the right to inherit, the unborn can be said to be a person in an equal sense, for the child born has no more rights with respect to inheritance. It makes more sense to say in an equal sense than "in the whole sense". As we interpret the common law, there could be an inheritance only for living heirs fixed at the time of death. If the unborn were deemed to be in existence, he or she would be a co-heir with born siblings. The born alive concept has to do, we believe, with the distribution of the decedent's estate in an orderly manner: if the

---

32 James C. Mohr, *Abortion in America* 200 el. ff.

33 *In Re Holthausen's Will.* 26 NYS 2d 140, 143 (Surrogate's Court N.Y. 1941). (Citation omitted.)

unborn were not born alive, it would be superfluous to probate an estate for the unborn also. In *Wade,* the Court was persuaded that the real purpose of the restrictive abortion laws was to protect maternal health, which we now state without fear of contradiction is false. Because of the subsequent investigative work of James C. Mohr, the conclusion now seems inescapable that the purpose of the Nineteenth Century laws was to protect the right to life of the unborn.

A corporation presents an example of a non-human being enjoying legal personality.[34]

By meeting the requirements of state law, this legal person has all of the rights available to other corporations, and they are substantial. As a practical matter, corporations may end up with rights greater than human beings.[35]

In 1886, the Supreme Court unanimously elevated corporations to the status of Fourteenth Amendment persons.[36] No rationale was given by the Court, but it seems from here that the single reason is that the corporation was a legal person: "Nor shall any state deprive any person of the equal protection of law." Any person meant any legal person. A Fourteenth Amendment person, then, is first of all a legal person under state law. As has been demonstrated, the unborn is a legal person having been given the right to life by virtue of Nineteenth Century state legislation. The unborn is consequently a Fourteenth Amendment person whose life cannot be deprived without due process nor without equal protection. From our vantage point, all legal persons are entitled to constitutional protections. This is demonstrated not only by the

---

[34] In *Doe v. Bolton,* 410 U.S. 179, 197 (1973), Justice Blackmun wrote: "It is to be remembered that the hospital is an entity and that it, too, has legal rights and legal obligations."

[35] See, e.g. Neb. Rev. Stat. §8-114 (Reissue of 1983) providing that only a corporation may conduct a bank.

[36] *Santa Clara County v. Southern Pacific RR.,* 118 U.S. 394 (1886). Former Justices Hugo L. Black and Wiliam O. Douglas have objected to this inclusion. See dissenting opinions in *Wheeling Steel Corp. v. Glander,* 337 U.S. 562, 576 (1949). *Connecticut General Life Ins. Co. v. Johnson,* 303 U.S. 77, 87 (1938). Compare: Howard Graham, "The Conspiracy Theory of the Fourteenth Amendment," 47 Yale L.J. 371 (1938) and 48 Yale L.J. 171 (1938).

corporation cases, but also by decisions dealing with illegitimates: "They are not non persons. They are humans, live, and have their being."[37]

It should be remembered that to be a legal person an entity need have but one right; thus an unborn child having the right to life is not required to have any other legal rights to be considered a legal person. John Locke maintained that the young were not at liberty because they had not acquired the use of reason. It can readily be envisioned in our society that legal rights are acquired only gradually by youth. Obvious examples are the rights to consume alcohol, to drive and to vote. The unborn need have none of these rights. There is but one necessary right, the right to life.

Earlier we discussed the unborn as a legal person because of having the right to inherit property, which must be respected by all. *Wade* infers otherwise. Assume that an unborn child, david, is eight weeks into development when his father dies, leaving david and david's mother the only heirs. In the good old days, david's mother could not have a legal abortion even if she wanted one, and nature willing, david would have been born and entitled to the inheritance.

Since 1973, were the mother desirous of being the sole heir, *Wade* is tailor-made. As easy as ABC, mother finds a willing physician and now david is turned into undavid that something should be done about the unwanted child, that something being abortion. In the example above, we demonstrated how a settled law of property could be suddenly overturned. If we alter our example so that the mother does not abort david, who is subsequently born alive, we have our own happy ending. While the inheritance is fine, this obviously is not a substitute for life.

In many states, one gets the right to drive at sixteen. If you kill the child at fifteen or younger, he or she will never get the right to drive. The same applies to the unborn. By killing david, one will as effectively deny the right to inherit as depriving the 15-year old the right to drive. In retrospect, it is not the loss of the right to drive or inherit that is so significant, but the right to life.

A point worth considering is that the right to property is meaningless without the attendant right to life. Before having the right to inherit property, it is logical that david should first have the right to life.

---

37   *Levy v. Louisiana*, 391 U.S. 68, 70 (1968).

For david to legally have the right to life the property right becomes insignificant, as life is the right to have other rights.[38]

From this we contend that life is the first right and must be recognized as such. You will recall that life always, with the exception of *Wade,* precedes liberty and property in the scheme recognizing these rights of a person.

RALEIGH FITKIN AND DRED SCOTT

The further we pursue the matter, more firm, becomes our conviction that the fate of the unborn need not rest upon a consensus of philosophers, theologians and physicians. Insofar as these diverse groups tend to ignore person as defined in the dictionary, insofar as they tend to ignore the essential classifications of living beings since the time of Aristotle they too can be disregarded.

It is much more logical to call the human unborn a human being than it is to call it an animal or vegetable. Science does not recognize potential human beings, potential animals, potential plants. *Roe v. Wade* is an affront to science, we suggest.

We can be sure that the physicians of yesteryear did, to the best of their ability, insure that the unborn would get legal protection from conception. With strange inconsistency, the law fully acknowledges the foetus in utero and its inherent rights, for civil purposes; while personally and as criminally affected, it fails to recognize it, and to its life as yet denies all protection.[39]

These are words from the American Medical Association and indicate that that body was seeking legal protection for the unborn prior to the time that equal protection was part of the Constitution. How can the Court rationally overlook this evidence?

Recalling *Raleigh Fitkin-Paul Morgan Memorial Hospital v. Anderson,*[40] we find that the right to life of the unborn child took precedence over the mother's religious liberty claim. That court recognized this as a basic legal right of the unborn child. Without citation

---

[38]   See *Furman v. Georgia,* 408 U.S. 238, 290 (Brennan, concurring).

[39]   410 U.S.

[40]   at 141-142.

to any statute, the court found the right to life. We would suggest that *Wade*, remaining still on this point, *sub silento* nullified *Raleigh Fitkin*. Thus, *Wade* is a prominent example of how the application of bad law leads to other bad laws. Since *Wade*, the unborn is subjected to his/ her mother's whims, be they high-minded, premised on the highlaw of religion, or any reason, kookie or not. Since *Wade*, juxtaposition reigns supreme over the country. It is now liberty, life and property, or liberty, property and life - the Court did not make it clear whether property or life was to be valued higher -that cannot be deprived without due process. In contortionist fashion, *Wade* was a coronation of Ms. Liberty triumphing over life.

Additionally, *Roe v. Wade* dramatically popularizes the unwanted child. While most physicians and most pregnant women are delighted with pregnancy, taking whatever steps are deemed beneficial to the unborn's life in the womb, the Court is singing the praises of the joy of abortion, the only civilized step to take.[41] If ever there existed a more blatant example of the denial of the equal protection of the laws in the United States, we have yet to find it. David lives while undavid is destroyed. Liberated woman denominated the unborn as unwanted. The Court, blind to the fact that this non-plant, non-animal was fully a human being because there existed no other classification, unscientifically measured the unborn as a potential human being, meaning not a human being. Cloaking Ms. Liberty with all the power it could muster, the Court stated that it took a "compelling interest" to unseat the Queen, but fetal life, mere potential life, a theory, fell short because it was not meaningful life. Hark! Spread the message to all these loonies who are overjoyed with their pregnancy: their unborn child is not meaningful. And hence the judicial blessing on the intentional elimination of the being that is merely potential, inferior and meaningless. The unborn may be classified as a person because it is a human being or other legal entity. As we know without doubt, the physicians visited the legislature urging the protection of human life from conception. In conferring the right to life, the legislators established legal personality. Legal personality should have been sufficient to create Fourteenth Amendment status. As was discussed in Part l, the unborn is a child; a child is a person. It necessarily

---

[41]   410 U.S. at 216 (Douglas, concurring).

follows that this unborn person should be entitled to life as are all other persons. *Dred Scott,* an emotional and excitable decision, suffered because the issue behind the scene was that the blacks were slaves which, as we have seen, violates John Locke's principles of liberty and property. We believe that any time one, by law, makes a man property, he is stating an inconsistency. As John Locke said, property is a right of man. Similarly, when one seeks to justify abortion, he argues with emotion rather than logic. Black "X" is a human being. For Locke, this black would have the right to life, liberty and property. If you violate this concept, trouble will brew eventually, as happened in the United States. The analogy is applicable to *Roe v. Wade.* When you afford the right to abort at will, you must necessarily, intellectually and emotionally, deny the unborn the status of person or human being. Thus, you are offended when someone claims this to be murder of the human being.[42] By denying the existence of human life, you can then justify abortion as the only civilized thing to do. But if you think through the dictionary meanings of person, you find that abortion is, in fact, the intentional destruction of a human being. Thus, no less authority than the dictionary makes the claim for liberal abortion a shambles.

Dred Scott was right on the Constitution and wrong on principles of life, liberty and property as described by Locke. *Wade,* by comparison, was wrong on the Constitution and wrong on Locke's principles. Slavery existed for centuries in this country. It is hoped that the abortion presence is destined for a much shorter stay.

PERSON IN THE WHOLE SENSE

Justice Blackmun: "In short, the unborn have never been recognized as persons in the whole sense."[43] We can find no previous case requiring status of person in the whole sense for a Fourteenth Amendment person. Why employ it against the unborn? Obviously, once again bias. A new rule just for the unborn. Texas made the unborn a person just as much as it was possible to do. The fact seems to be *person in the whole sense* is a phrase manufactured by the liberal abortion mentality to deny the

---

42   Daniel Callahan, *Abortion: Law, Choice and Morality* 4.
43   410 U.S. at 162.

unborn constitutional status. If not in the whole sense, then in what sense? The Court was silent on this point. Just as was the case with *potential* human being, the Court employed creativity to describe and deny the unborn.

The illegitimates were certainly not "persons in the whole sense," as they were made non persons by the state legislature.[44] But they were nevertheless protected by the Equal Protection Clause.

In objecting to Justice Blackmun's phrase that the unborn was not a person in the whole sense, we rely also on the dictionary. As we have seen, person means a human being or other entity possessing legal rights and duties. To be a legal person, it is sufficient for the human being or entity to have one legal right. There has never been a requirement that the human being or other entity have two or five or any plural number of rights. The unborn is claiming two, the right to life and the right to inherit, this latter right affecting and actually benefiting a very tiny percentage of unborn. Assuming, as we must, that the legislators intended to give the right to life to the unborn in the Nineteenth Century, and they used language in their laws that were consistent with this intent, they created legal persons. We can find no Anglo-American source calling for a multiplication of rights to constitute a legal person.

"Sense" has many definitions in *Webster's Ninth New Collegiate Dictionary*, but the one that fits here best is "a meaning conveyed or intended: IMPORT, SIGNIFICATION: *esp.:* one of a set of meanings a word or phrase may bear esp. as segregated in a dictionary entry."[45] The key point is the sense of a thing means that it is just one of a possible set. In our example above, the legislators deemed the unborn a person in the sense that the unborn was a "human being" or a "three choice definition human being." Given the rigorous campaigning of various medical personnel, it is strongly arguable that the legislators deemed the unborn as a human being and not some "other legal entity" and legislated the right from conception to this burgeoning legal person.

---

44   *Levy v. Louisiana.* 391 U.S. 68,70 (1968). See text at *19 supra.*

45   By permission. From p. 1071 Webster's Ninth New Collegiate Dictionary ©1987 by Merriam-Webster Inc., publisher of the Merriam-Webster® Dictionaries.

"Whole" means "constituting the total sum or undiminished entirety: ENTIRE <owns the _____island>.[46] Sense, as we have noted, means one of a set; whole would suggest the entire set. In other words, the Court reasons that since the unborn is not recognized as having the entire set of rights that other legal entities, specifically human beings, may have, that the Court was reluctant to classify the unborn as a Fourteenth Amendment person. To be a person in the whole sense, the person would have to have every single legal right, suggests *Wade*. Infants do not qualify as they probably do not have (or need) religious freedom; they certainly cannot vote or legally operate motor vehicles. Young teenagers do not qualify as they are without the right to vote. Their sixth amendment rights do not equal that of adults as they do not have the same right to a jury trial in juvenile delinquency proceedings.[47] *Wade* teaches us that men are not persons in the whole sense, as they physically are unable to claim the right to abort nor can they constitutionally prohibit it. Corporations are not persons in the whole sense because they cannot vote for congressmen or in any other government election, nor can a corporation be given a driver's license. Illegitimates, according to the Supreme Court, were made non persons by the state legislators, obviously depriving them of status of person in the whole sense. Women were not originally persons in the whole sense, having been denied the right to vote, not having property rights for a period of time. They have made a push for equality and it has been successful to some extent. We have seen no proclamation that full equality has been achieved. Thus, women are deprived of the "whole-sense-person" status.

For the Court to take self-satisfaction over the unborn's status as not a person in the whole sense is blatantly unfair. No one is a person in the whole sense. Whole sense makes no sense. But it was applied to the unborn. The abortion cases are unparalleled. Prior to the abortion decisions, there has been no single case depriving an entity of rights because the entity was not a person in the whole sense. Not a single case on the Fourteenth Amendment or any other area of the law prescribed

---

[46] By permission. From p. 1347 \Webster's Ninth New Collegiate Dictionary ©1987 by Merriam-Webster Inc., publisher of the Merriam-Webster® Dictionaries.

[47] See *McKeiver v. Pennsylvania*, 403 U.S. 528 (1971).

succor only for. the person in the whole sense. The unborn was thus denied Fourteenth Amendment status or account of an unprecedented and impossible standard: there is no person in the whole sense. We ask again, were the crusading physicians of a century ago in fundamental error? If so, does not someone owe womankind an apology for violating women's rights all these years? Is a belated apology in order from today's American Medical Association? While we have our own opinions, we eagerly await word from the prestigious AMA.

It thus comes to pass that the Court, in declaring that the unborn was not a person in the whole sense, means that legally the unborn is a person in no sense. While we cannot put much stock in "the person in the whole sense" jargon, we can visualize that *Wade* has created a new classification of person, which is superperson, who now towers over and above the male in terms of constitutional rights. Superperson has fundamental rights under the Constitution, marking the first time, the only time that one sex has acquired fundamental rights specifically denied the other. With the emergence of superperson, it is adios to the tiny Texas legal person who obviously is short on many rights: religion, speech, driving, and the only one that matters, life. Superperson decides what is life and what is just a theory of life, the most awesome power ever bestowed on any segment of society. She is superperson because she has constitutional rights unavailable to a male.

RECAP

A considerable portion of our argument on the status of the unborn has been based on the dictionary, which is based upon science. We, in turn, believe that a fatal flaw in *Wade* was ineffectively limiting consideration of the unborn as a "human being" as determined by a consensus of philosophers, theologians and physicians. Each side spoke in its own circle without being able to reach an agreement. The Court's analysis of the legal person was all too brief and unclear and inconclusive. It seems probable that if reasonable minds can come to grips with the definitions, including the three-choice definition, the inferior human being and the legal entity, the next analysis of abortion by the Supreme Court will be more fruitful. Hopefully, the Court will give a more definitive idea of person and will not hesitate to use the phrase human being.

This would be in accordance with the words of John Locke in *An Essay Concerning Understanding: Wisdom, grace, glory, etc.,* are words frequent enough in every man's mouth; but if a great many of those who use them should be asked what they mean by them, they would be at a stand, and not know what to answer: a plain proof, that, though they have learned these sounds, and have them ready at their tongues' ends, yet there are no determined ideas laid up in their minds, which are to be expressed to others by them.

So These words of Locke seem to foreshadow *Wade.* What else can we say about a Court that presumed to answer questions concerning the Fourteenth Amendment while neglecting the basic chore of defining person or defining life? If the Court is going to continue to deny the unborn Fourteenth Amendment status, is it asking too much for the justices to identify that person and thereby point out the deficiencies in the unborn? If the Court is unwilling to employ the dictionary in quest of the constitutional status of the unborn, and if the Court is going to ignore science, the Court can expect a hue and cry from the advocates of the unborn complaining of continuing unfairness. Of course, the possibility exists that the present court will continue to deny the unborn the right to be heard, leaving the assignment for a future court.

Roe v. Wade seems to be a case in which the Court voted for abortion on demand and only afterwards attempted to devise rationale to sustain its position. Precious little time or thought was extended to the plight of the unborn. Despite words to the contrary, the Court was emotionally entangled with the woman who was carrying an unwanted child.

It was a court that mangled history, that failed to inquire into the meaning of life, and that gave no serious inquiry into the constitutional understanding of person. Did the Supreme Court ask for consensus from philosophers, theologians and physicians before pronouncing the corporation a Fourteenth Amendment person? Of course not. Until the 1960's, each of the fifty states was able to abide by a restrictive abortion law. In 1973, liberty or privacy carried the day. The unwanted unborn was tagged as potential life and was branded as meaningless life: make it unwanted and get rid of it. The words of Patrick Henry can be slightly altered: Give her liberty and give me death; for every abortion results in the death of an unborn child. It is not out of line to speak of abortion resulting in death. We get the same picture when looking at Article 1191, as the Court must have on numerous instances: "the life of the fetus or embryo shall [not] be destroyed." Article 1191 was referring to death which the Court did not bring itself to discuss.

The alternative to *Wade* begins with a case in which the unborn child has full legal representation from the outset. A study of history reveals what *Wade* did not find: that the purpose of the Nineteenth Century laws was to protect the life of the unborn, one goes further than "human being" in seeking out the meaning of person. Not being a vegetable or animal, the unborn is really a human' being. Alternatively, the unborn is a legal entity who has been given the right to life by the state legislature. The unwanted unborn, nestled in a hostile environment, is an inferior human being destined to be.[48]

The *Wade*-approved approach results in well over 1.5 million human beings being deprived of life without ceremony each year _ without due process. Those unfortunate human beings who are inferior because they are unloved and unwanted are killed off by individuals judging their own case. As described by John Locke:..where men may be judges in their own case . ..it is easy to be imagined that he who was so unjust as to do his brother an injury will scarce be so just as to condemn himself for I Substitute "she" and "her" for "he" and "him", and "unborn child" for "brother" and you have an accurate picture of abortion where the Court has licensed women to be judges in their own cases and medical doctors to be executioners. Some of these licensed men and women change their mind after they have performed many abortions.[49]

As usurpation is the exercise of power which another has a right to, so tyranny is the exercise of power beyond right, which nobody can have a right to; and this is making use of the power anyone has in his hands, not for the good of those who are under it, but for his own private, separate advantage.[50]

---

[48] *John Locke, Concerning Human Understanding III. X,3.*

[49] John Locke, *Concerning Civil Government, Second Essay* II, 13.

[50] See Bernard N. Nathanson who admits to presiding over 60,000 abortion deaths and now relates the wrongness of it all. *Aborting America* xi (Garden City, New York: Doubleday & Co. 1979).

"Raw judicial power"[51] gives approval of the woman to invade and destroy her unborn. The pregnant woman and her use of raw power through her physician is tyrannical in the Lockean sense, as no one has the right to take that life, neither woman nor doctor.

Nobody can have a right to abort an unborn child, save when it is necessary to preserve maternal life. Further on the same subject from Locke:

[The proud and ambitious tyrant doth think his kingdom and people are only ordained for satisfaction of his desires and unreasonable appetites....[52]

Locke, of course, although having a high regard for life, defining liberty broadly and respecting estate or property, abhorred abortion _ it was against God's law, immoral.[53]

When the law states to pregnant women that they should decide whether their pregnancies are wanted or unwanted and act accordingly, the law is bestowing the power to act arbitrarily and capriciously. Then inferior unborn _ those who are unwanted _ are denied the equal protection of the laws. It is not fair to target those who are unwanted to some degree. Born children are all wanted or unwanted to some extent, as indicated by extensive reports of child abuse. No one would suggest a good riddance to the unwanted born child. Why should it be different prior to birth? If one contemplates the cause of the unborn, unwanted child, one reaches the conclusion that the system of giving the pregnant woman unbridled control over that life is unacceptable. The case for the woman collapses. Until then, tyranny terrorizes the landscape.

THE FOURTEENTH AMENDMENT
PERSON A HUMAN BEING?

Should the words "person" and "life" in the Fourteenth Amendment be given a broad or a restrictive meaning? Of course, the *Wade* Court did not tell us. The words of former Justice Frankfurter, quoted earlier,

---

[51] John Locke, Concerning Civil Government, Second Essay II, 13.

[52] 410 ·u..at 222 (White, concurring).

[53] John Locke, *Concerning Civil Government, Second Essay* XVIII, 200.

seem to suggest an expanded view of "life."[54] A noted commentator prior to *Wade* stated that the Court already had given the word "person" the broadest possible meaning.[55] We are rather persuaded that where the Court to consider the matter in direct terms, the Court would opt for an expansive view of both words - assuming that it could ignore emotional sob stories about the unwanted child.

In the *Vuitch* case, cited in *Wade,* the Supreme Court used a standard dictionary and gave the broadest definition possible for the word health.[56]

We recall also, from Part I, that life should be valued higher than liberty in the Fourteenth Amendment.

If we were pressed to isolate the single most crucial mistake in the error-plagued *Roe v. Wade,* it would be the failure of the Court to define the Fourteenth Amendment person. As already noted, it had already been given the broadest possible meaning. Why the reversal of course? Is it one more example of bias demonstrated against the unborn? If we do not know what a Fourteenth Amendment person is, we do not have a standard to judge whether the unborn fits in.

Perhaps we can help fill in the void in *Wade.* We know that the Amendment was written with the Negro in mind. But on May 10, 1886, the Court handed down two decisions with broad repercussions. First, there was *Yick Wo v. Hopkins,* which held that the equal protection clause was not to benefit Negroes alone:

These provisions are universal in their application, to all persons within the territorial jurisdiction, without regard to any differences of race, of color or of nationality; and the equal protection of the laws is a pledge of the protection of equal laws.[57]

With respect to the second case, the following is reported early in the opinion of Santa Clara County v. Southern Pacific RR:

---

54   410 U.S. at 169 (concurring opinion of Justice Stewart).'See text at notes 105-106 Part I *supra.*

55   Norman J. Small, Editor *The Constitution of the United States of America* 1281 (Washington, D.C.: U.S Government Printing Office 1964).

56   402 U.S. at 71-72. See also 410 U.S. at 207 (concurring opinion, Chief Justice Burger).

57   118 U. S. 356, 369 (1886)

MR. CHIEF JUSTICE WAITE said: The Court does not wish to hear argument on the question whether the provision in the Fourteenth Amendment to the Constitution, which forbids a state to deny to any person within its jurisdiction to the equal protection of the laws, applied to these corporation. We are all of the opinion that it does.[58]

In *Glona v. American Guaranty & Liability Ins. Co.*, the Court referred to the companion case of *Levy v. Louisiana*, and stated:

...the present case is different from the Levy case, where by mere accident of birth the innocent, although illegitimate, child was made a "nonperson" by the legislature, when it came to recovery for damages for the wrongful death of his mother.

If we go back to *Levy*, we find the following spoken:

We start from the premise that illegitimate children are not "non persons". They are humans, live, and have their being. They are clearly "persons" within the meaning of the Equal Protection Clause of the Fourteenth Amendment.[59]

What these cases share in common with *Santa Clara County, is* the status as a legal person. That is the only conceivable rational basis for including the corporation in the Fourteenth Amendment. In *Levy* and *Glona,* the out-of-wedlock relationships resulted in the legal status of non persons, no rights. It was the equal protection clause that swept away the barriers, and in effect made the illegitimates legal persons under state law.

We would submit that based upon the four decisions cited above, there is no magic in the Fourteenth Amendment person, no mystique. Rather, plainly and simply, a Fourteenth Amendment person is a legal person. And it is not always a matter of what is legal. We must also look to what is biological:

To say that the test of equal protection should be the "legal" rather than the biological relationship is to avoid the issue. For the Equal Protection Clause necessarily limits the authority of a State to draw such "legal" lines as it chooses.[60]

---

[58]   118 u.s. 394, 396 (1886).

[59]   391 u.s. 68, 70 (1978). (Footnotes omitted.)

[60]   391 U.S. at 75-76.

While it is not essential that the legal person be a human being, it would be more difficult for the Court to deny Fourteenth Amendment status for the human.

In putting forth the proposition that a Fourteenth Amendment person is a legal person, we have done more than the *Wade* Court did. We have provided a definition. Most of the time the legal person is also a human being.

If the definition that we have suggested is incorrect, or if there is a better one, please provide it. Until then, we will go with what we have.

THE ABA, APHA AND AMA: EXPERTS?

Earlier we posited the need for the unborn to have separate representation. The representation would have to ascertain and be able to demonstrate first of all that *Roe v. Wade* is fraught with error and thus subject to be toppled; second, the representative would have to establish with scientific evidence that the unborn is a human being from conception and not an animal or plant; third, the representative would attempt to persuade the courts at all levels that the inquiry is a scientific or medical question and nothing else. Consequently, the representative of the unborn must be ever-vigilant concerning testimony from the likes of philosophers, theologians and other non-scientists.

There is a similar danger in focusing on particular groups and ascertaining their "position". Thus, with the American Bar Association, we have an objection. It is utterly irrelevant what the non-scientific lawyers think on abortion. They are not qualified to give an expert opinion, but this is the effect of *Wade*. Were there to be a trial on abortion in the local courthouse, we do not believe that either side would call an attorney as an expert witness. If so, the attorney would likely be laughed out of court. If the attorney in isolation is not an expert, the convening of several hundred means there are several hundred non-experts gathered. Their "position" is not worthy of consideration when the subject is the Constitution. If the retort is that the opinion is not expert, then the response is that every other non-scientific American should likewise have a vote or "position" reportable, which, of course, is absurd.

Next, we examine the "position" of the American Public Health Association. Who makes up this organization? Is it only physicians or are there others? What is the function of the Association? How long has it been in existence? What is the makeup of the Executive Board? How is the APHA related to the American Medical Association? Did the Executive Board come to a conclusion that the unborn did not constitute human life? If so, what criteria were used? Was it scientifically based or was it colored by religious and philosophical considerations? What is the relationship between the Executive Board and the other members of the Association? Did the member's request or demand that these views be promulgated or was this simply initiated by the Executive Board? Does the APHA represent a fair cross section of all physicians? Is the APHA simply one of the leaders in the liberal abortion movement, and not a disinterested bystander?[61] The position of the APHA, if it has any relevance, is that of an expert. Fundamental fairness, of course, should require that the opponent, the unborn, should be able to cross-examine the members of the Executive Board. The difficulty with taking the opinions of any organization is this lack of ability to cross examine the formulators. For this reason, we object to the position of the APHA. This same consideration is why we emphasize that the primary evidence offered by the unborn should be views of single individuals.

With respect to the American Medical Association, we run into some of the same difficulties as with the APHA. If we are going to receive the views of the AMA, we should theoretically be able to cross-examine every physician in the country. Obviously, that would be somewhat unwieldy, to say the least. The unborn probably does not have a treasure chest to finance such an undertaking.

We have indicated above that the best evidence is the expert opinion of the physician or other scientist. The view of the physicians as a whole, not subject to cross-examination, is of secondary value. Where every physician in the country to vote for restrictive abortion laws, we would not necessarily have satisfactory proof of the unborn's scientific status. But since the AMA of yesterday did take a vote and did reach a consensus, we believe that the physicians in the country are one group who should be heard. Our own inclination is to register a certain amount of distrust

---

[61] *Glona v. American Guaranty & Liability Ins. Co.* See Bernard N. Nathanson, *Aborting America* 54, 146, wherein the tie-in with the liberal abortion movement is suggested.

to the action taken by delegates of organizations who often may not accurately reflect the views of the constituency. For this reason, we are agreeing that the physicians should be heard from, but that we should go to the source, the local medical societies. In this manner, each physician will be able to project an opinion. As we have noted, the physicians of a century ago were leaders on the abortion issue, while the modern counterparts have taken the role of followers. We find their unwillingness to lead in 1970 and subsequent years to be a curious position inasmuch as within their midst are the only real experts in the field. As advocates of the unborn, we are relying on physicians to advance the cause of the unborn. If the physicians cannot be counted on to take a stand on the humanity of the unborn, there is no one left. We repeat in clear terms what has been suggested: the medical scientists must come to grips with the unborn beings who are either human or something else. If the physicians are unable to classify the unborn as humans, the response must be then what kind of being? The unborn either constitutes human life or some other form of life. If not human, then what? Only the medical scientists and perhaps other scientists are qualified to answer.

In any event, we believe it is unfair and perhaps misleading for the Supreme Court to put forth the position of the likes of the AMA, APHA and ABA. There was no showing that the votes of the leaders of these organizations represented the views of the rank and file. Moreover, there was no method made available to cross-examine them as to how their views were formulated, what factors were considered, whether they were influenced by the constituency, etc. By and large, the "organization" does not make for an expert. It is only the individuals who can be experts because only they can be cross-examined. The Court, in relying on these organizational experts, was prejudiced against the unborn's case. It is one thing to assert that a church has an official doctrine put forth by the church leaders, but it is quite another matter to attribute positions to other loose-knit organizations. And if the Supreme Court did not imperceptibly clothe these three organizations with the status of expert witness, what function precisely did the organizations serve? The reader's attention is called to Part I wherein we discussed the common law. There the accepted experts were the great common law writers. Additional authority was the American state courts. The *Wade* Court rejected all this authority and grasped at the meanderings of Cyril C. Means who seemed to place much emphasis on the fact that Edward Coke was a Catholic and had exceptionally strong feelings on abortion. What Means and the Court fail to realize is that in Seventeenth Century England, Catholics, a minority, were not inclined to be any more severe on abortion than would members of the Church of England. Par for the course, *Wade* superficially and casually cast aside the real experts on the common law.

THE REAL EXPERTS

Area of Speciality: _____

_____

We have suggested that perhaps all physicians are not interested in abortion. If they are disinterested and have made no attempt to become aware of and to keep apprised of developments in the field, then we would reject them as experts. Do all physicians have a view on abortion? It is our suspicion that the views of the physicians are a mixed bag. We believe that in this age of specialization, many physicians who do not deal with abortion in their own practice will have no opinion. In order to ascertain the position of physicians on abortion, we believe it is too simplistic to ask whether they are in favor or opposed; more important is the inquiry whether the physician speaks as an expert or non-expert. We have a brief survey to be given to physicians at local meetings. The responding physician need mark one of five statements, or write in his or her own if the five are not satisfactory. The physician is asked to identify himself or herself by specialty.

SURVEY OF PHYSICIANS ON ABORTION

1. I believe I qualify as an expert on the subject of abortion, and I also believe the unborn is a human being from conception, and therefore abortion is wrong except to save the life of the pregnant woman.
2. I believe I qualify as an expert on the subject of abortion, and I believe that the unborn is not a human being from conception, and therefore abortion is not wrong.

3. I do not believe I am an expert on abortion, but I believe that abortion is wrong unless necessary to preserve the life of the pregnant woman.
4. I do not believe that I am an expert on abortion, but I do not believe abortion is wrong.
5. I do not have an opinion, or I do not wish to express an opinion. Other (if you have not marked I through 5), please state your view:
6. In a survey of this kind, we are not subjecting the survey to cross-examination. Nevertheless, we believe the survey has some validity in first of all ascertaining the views of the physicians and secondly, for bringing us closer to an answer as to actually how many of the physicians consider themselves experts. The results might be surprising. This was a post-*Wade* survey...

THE COUNCIL BLUFFS PHYSICIANS

We took our survey to the physicians of Council Bluffs, Iowa, a city with a population of approximately 56,000. There is no special significance to the selection of Council Bluffs other than it is the author's place of residence. There are two hospitals in Council Bluffs, and representatives from both have indicated that abortions are not performed in their facilities. Council Bluffs has no clinics providing abortion services, but two such facilities are located in Omaha, Nebraska, across the Missouri River.

One pro-life group, Council Bluffs Right to Life, is organized in the city. According to Joyce Farrington, coordinator, the organization has not participated in picketing the abortion clinics in Omaha as has been done by Omaha right to life members. The Council Bluffs Right to Life has a mailing list of 300, attendance at meetings being little more than 12 or 13.

We have been unable to discover any feminist groups in Council Bluffs.

All in all, it is our impression that Council Bluffs is essentially a conservative city, conservative in the sense that the population is more or less indifferent to the dilemma imposed by abortion and is not uncomfortable with the dictates of *Roe v. Wade* and many are equally accepting of the pro-life view. But few get demonstrative about their views.

In giving the survey to the Council Bluffs physicians, we were anticipating a conservative response, with conservative meaning passively accepting one of the two basic positions, right to life or acceptability of abortion in most instances, without being very vocal about it. Our survey was not designed to measure "conservatism" as we have defined it versus the more radicalism or vocalism.

Surveys were sent to 90 physicians, and 28 responded by mail. Six bypassed the first five choices. In selecting "other", their comments were such that we thought they could be included in the first five categories. One physician wrote: "I would have marked #4 above, but I felt that this is too liberal while #3 is slightly too strict." We have placed this one and two others in #4 when they seemed to be for abortions in circumstances other than to protect maternal life. One physician would not allow abortion even to protect maternal life. We were not so much concerned with the physicians' views as we were with whether they were considering themselves experts.

The breakdown after we "unscrambled" the six "other" votes:

4	1.
0	2.
9	3.
9	4.

I believe I qualify as an expert on the subject of abortion, and I also believe the unborn is a human being from conception, and therefore abortion is wrong except to save the life of the pregnant woman.

I believe I qualify as an expert on the subject of abortion, and I believe that the unborn is not a human being from conception, and therefore abortion is not wrong.

I do not believe I am an expert on abortion, but I believe that abortion is wrong unless necessary to preserve the life of the pregnant woman.[62] I do not have an opinion, or I do not wish to express an opinion. Combining the 4 in #1 with the 9 in #3, we get a total of 13 for restrictive abortion, which compared with 9 favoring a more liberal policy. As we mentioned in the previous section, this is probably not a significant vote because most of these physicians are admitting that they are not experts on the subject.

The 6 who selected #5 present a more interesting figure, we believe. While we may be inclined to interpret this as meaning 6 are not interested in abortion, at least one selected this because of the indeterminacy of the basic question and directed to us: "first the answer to when life begins."

Some did not indicate their area of speciality. But we heard from at least one of the following: orthopedic surgeon, family practice, general practice, pediatrics, urology, obstetrics-gynecology, ophthalmology, internal medicine, general surgery, neurosurgery, pathology, cardiology, and psychiatry.

We were most interested in who were the experts. The following language was used in the cover letter with the survey: "I am not defining 'expert'. You will have to decide for yourself whether you believe you are qualified to appear in court on the subject of abortion." We anguished over whether to define expert, but finally let the physicians reach their own decision. On this subject, one physician raised the question of experts in pointed fashion: "What is an expert? One who is paid for providing these services? Or spends time supporting [the] pro-life position?" Those four claiming to be experts identified themselves as "ob. & gyn." (two), family practice, and psychiatry. Each of these could be characterized as claiming to be pro-life experts, with no experts on the other side of the fence. One of these four indicated a willingness to accept abortion in a case where rape was documented. We cannot account for any reason that no Council Bluffs physician has come forward claiming to be an expert for the liberal abortion side.

What we find fascinating is that less than 15% of the physicians are claiming to be experts. That means the reverse or 85% were asking to

---

62   *Glona v. American Guaranty & Liability Ins. Co. See Bernard N. Nathanson, Aborting America 54, 146, wherein the tie-in with the liberal abortion movement is suggested.*

be deemed non-experts. When we consider that less than 15% of the Council Bluffs physicians consider themselves experts, let us project this same figure across the country. While we do not contend that our sample of 28 physicians is sufficient to extrapolate scientifically on a national level, the Council Bluffs experience does show that many physicians are not experts on the subject of abortion, at least they do not claim to be.

Return with us to the House of Delegates of the American Medical Association in 1970. Were those physicians who voted to comply with state abortion laws all experts? The Council Bluffs experience would lead us to believe not. If not, how do we know they made an opinion achieved by expertise? Similarly, with respect to the Supreme Court, did they make yet another error in relying on the vote of the AMA 1970? We believe our Council Bluffs survey suggests the probability that the action taken by the AMA does simply not measure the careful analysis of expert scientists on the question of abortion. Two final thoughts. One, we have not proclaimed that any of the Council Bluffs four are in fact experts on the subject of abortion. About the only way to ascertain this would be to inject them into the courtroom setting where the witness by his own testimony would have to establish his credentials as an expert. Two, the reader will note that we have cited no Harris or Gallup polls on the subject of abortion nor have we attempted to procure one in Council Bluffs. Virtually all of us -this author included- are non-experts and consequently, our personal views, while important to us personally, are insignificant in the larger scheme of things: is abortion right? Even if 10,000 non-experts voiced a unanimous opinion, we would have no basis for judging whether this 10,000 sample was alright or all wet. The next time you see the results of such a survey, you can view it with askance. While the polls are certainly harmless in themselves and may accurately assess public opinion at a given time, as time changes, there is often a shift in opinion. What is right is right, what is wrong is wrong, regardless of the swings or drifts in public sentiment. By contrast, we do not believe that true expert opinion will shift with changing popular opinion. Nor do we believe that just because one is very vocal the person is not necessarily an expert.

EVIDENCE

While it should suffice to establish that the unborn is a legal person, human or not, the *Wade* experience dictates that we go further. The point of our discussion is to be able to establish in court that the unborn is a constitutional person. The only method we know to accomplish this is by medical testimony. Seemingly, any physician will affirm the proposition that living beings are vegetable, animal or human. This gives us a place to begin.

We would suggest that most physicians will not know from their own observations and experiences that the unborn from conception is in fact a human being. This information would likely be obtained from a medical text or treatise. The *Wade* Court stated: "They outline at length and in detail the well-known facts of fetal development." Well-known by whom? We do not believe these facts were well-known by the members of the Supreme Court. How would the Court have come to know them prior to *Wade?* They had no case prior to *Wade* involving the unborn. We would express our belief that the facts of fetal development are not even known to all physicians, many of whose professional responsibilities are not involved with unborn children.

On this subject, we would ask whether the Supreme Court considered the well-known facts of fetal development as evidence in *Wade.* If so, it got the evidence in a very unorthodox manner. It is generally live witnesses who present their evidence in court subject to cross-examination. If they rely on written materials, they can be cross-examined on that basis. If this was not evidence, we ask what evidence did the Court rely upon in concluding that the physicians would not reach a consensus? We note that the district court did not report the taking or the reliance upon medical or scientific evidence. In the case in which the unborn was not a party and not a scintilla of medical evidence was taken, the lower court stated there were no contested issues of fact.[63] Once again, the Supreme Court's own words and actions show a court that forgot to take testimony on a disputed fact, the status of the unborn. In unprecedented fashion>, the United States Supreme Court compounded this error by accepting arguments of amici as an apparently

---

[63] See *Roe V. Wade,* 314 F. Supp. 1217, 1224 (D.C. Tex. 1970).

acceptable alternative. The only other suggestion of controverted facts was the polarization of the AMA in 1970 as reported by the Court. Is there no end to the errors of *Wade?*

In any event, the expert witness may rely on texts and treatises, as is common for experts in any field. The physician may be asked: What evidence exists to cause you to believe that the unborn is a human being? What evidence suggests that the unborn is an animal? A plant or vegetable? Does the scientific community speak of potential humans, animals or vegetables? If so, what is meant by the terms? Which writers, if any, call the unborn human animal or thing? Has the scientific community since the time of Aristotle acquired a wealth of knowledge about the unborn that was unknown? In states in which the rigid Nineteenth Century laws were in effect at the time of *Wade,* the evidence should carry back to the last century. We believe a court could take judicial notice of the proceedings of the American Medical Association in 1857 and 1871 as reported in *Roe v. Wade.* In each jurisdiction, it would be up to the unborn's advocate to present evidence that the local medical society lobbied for a given law claiming the unborn to be human, and that the legislature responded favorably. Proceeding in this manner, foundation will. have been laid to demonstrate that the unborn was considered a human being by the Nineteenth Century physicians and that the unborn, whether human or not, was made a legal person by the lawmakers. If records are not available to establish clearly the purpose of the Nineteenth Century laws, it can still be argued that the effect of the laws was. to protects human life from conception, that the unborn were made legal persons. In those states in which the Nineteenth Century laws were modified because of considerations of physical defects and mental deficiencies and by rape and incest, it would seem that the activities from ihe last century would be relevant, as would be the evidence of modern changes. The contention is that the law was intended to protect all unborn life in the last century, while the more recent changes have been a retreat. The argument, of course, would be that the changes have been wrong for failing to protect life universally. In states such as New York where all protection of the unborn was withdrawn, the Nineteenth Century legislation would appear to be irrelevant inasmuch as the most recent law did not recognize the unborn as legal entities. In New York, evidence would be only the medical expert or experts. We believe the opposition, of course, would likely present evidence that the purpose of the law was only to protect women. We would not also attempt to submit the results of surveys of the local medical association even if they were recent. These polls arguably have been made relevant by the stance taken by the medical associations in the past century. It is secondary evidence and is not a substitute for the medical expert subject to cross-examination. As the Council Bluffs experience shows, many physicians are not experts, and it is in error to so consider them. The main point of such surveys would be to demonstrate that the average physician is not an expert and that his or her view is entitled to no weight. The opposition may, of course, call witnesses to counter the unborn's. But under cross examination, he or she should be subjected to the same questions as your own expert. Are the opinions based upon science? Are they based upon some recognized scientific writings? Are living things classified as human, animal or vegetable? If not, how are they classified? Are not physicians limited to practicing medicine upon humans? Do veterinarians ever treat the unborn? Is the unborn an animal? Which one? Perhaps a wolf? If the unborn is a plant, which one? Does the unborn have human-like features? Which plants have human like qualities? Does a physician consult a horticulturalist as to the care of the unborn? And so on.

We believe that the well-versed medical doctor who opines that the unborn is a human being from conception will fare much better than the physician who does not know or who states the contrary. The trial court will have to evaluate the battle of the experts just as does the court on a daily basis in other kinds of cases. Back to *Wade*. Recalling Justice Blackmun's enchantment with those trained in medicine, philosophy and religion arriving at a consensus, we hope that our prior discussions have removed the unborn from the shackles of the philosophers and theologians. We must go one step further and ask that the search for consensus, even among physicians, be abandoned. In its place, we would substitute the notion of accepting the expert's' testimony which appears to be more credible, as happens in court day in and day out. For example, if Expert "A" were influenced primarily by considerations of religion or philosophy, the trial judge should take that into account, recognizing that he is not getting a scientific opinion. For a second example, Expert "A" does not read the scientific materials available and rely upon them; the value of the opinion should be judged accordingly. So far - all the way up to and including *Roe v. Wade* - the scientific basis for the validity of the unborn as a human being has not been adjudicated. *Byrn v. New York*

City Hosp. Corp[64] raised the issue but was ignored by the Supreme Court. *Roe v. Wade, as* we have noted, was totally lacking in medical testimony. The Court took a premature position in regarding the issue as unsolvable without waiting to hear from medical experts. Surely written accounts and treatises are not adequate substitutes for live witnesses. Did the Court invent another rule only for the unborn to the effect that witnesses are immaterial in this one instance? In virtually every sphere of law where expert witnesses come into play, there is a dispute between the experts. Judges and juries have been adept in dealing with them. Why all of a sudden, when the subject is abortion, is it *assumed* that the experts will be hopelessly divided so that no resolution can be forthcoming? While *Wade* goes through the motions of considering medical evidence, a close scrutiny reveals that the Court did not do so, making yet another error.

One additional argument relates to the American Medical Association. In 1857 and 1871 it voted to protect the unborn human life. In 1967 and again in 1970, the AMA acted inconsistently with the last century's physicians. But they did not squarely face the issue of a century ago. To the American Medical Association of 1987, we ask does the unborn constitute human life? Is the unborn a human being? If not, tell us what kind. We believe the argument can be made that the modern AMA has not quite arrived at the issue of the humanity of the unborn. Thus, we conclude they have not repudiated intellectually the express view of the AMA in 1871, even though they have taken votes and acted as if they have rejected the human unborn. Consequently, the argument can be made with some force that the AMA has never officially changed its views on the unborn since the last century. How many members of the AMA are experts on abortion, we wonder.

Appeal dismissed 410 U.S. 940 (1973). *Byrn* was pre-*Wade* and we have no reason to believe that the Court considered it carefully. The case suffered from a lack of cross-examination of its expert witnesses. *Wade* does seem to indicate thatl if the human-ness of the unborn were established, the unborn would be a Fourteenth Amendment person, contrary to that case's holding. *Byrn* did nothing to dispel the notion that philosophers and theologians are as valuable as physicians.

---

[64] While some might believe that *Byrn v. New York City Health and Hosp. Corp.*, 281 NE 2d 887 (1972)..

WADE IN COLLAPSE

The posh arguments of the pro-abortion contingency amount to little. The emotional appeal of Justice Blackmun for abortion on request is thus sapped of all vitality. What was dreaded by the *Wade majority* is the worst of all worlds for women unhappily pregnant. As stated in *Wade, pregnancy* and childbirth "may force upon the woman a distressful life and future."[65] With the reversal of *Wade, her* distress cannot be prevented, but she does have the alternative of giving the child up for adoption, thereby short-circuiting her bleak future so that her distress need only last the nine-month period of gestation. *Wade* correctly remarked that pregnancy "may tax the physical and mental health of the mother,"[66] but solicitude for life of the unborn takes precedence over health considerations." The distress for all concerned, associated with the unwanted child,"[67] will have to be endured. Abuse of a child, born or unborn, is obviously a hindrance to the child's life or limb. Justice Blackmun ushered in abortion as a solution to the unwanted child. If he was correct, we should only have wanted children born since 1973. We would expect all of our youngsters who were allowed to be born to be wanted. But abortion has failed to live up to its implied promise that the unwanted born child would be a statistic from history. On the contrary, the numbers of instances of child abuse is monumental and growing each year.[68] Surely one would not abuse a wanted child! Pregnancy and birth could constitute "a continuing stigma of unwed motherhood."[69] If society honored the vows as signifying "until death do us part," the point of the Court might be well taken. But in the United States in recent years, wedlock is not a forever thing in numerous instances, and

---

[65] 410 U.S. al 153.

[66] *Id.*

[67] *Id.*

[68] Reported child neglect and abuse cases in the United States: U.S. Bureau of the Census. *Statistical Abstract of the United States* (1986) (106th Edition) 172 (Washington D.C. 1985). At the same time. abortion statistics seemed to be holding more or less steady. *Id.* at 67:

[69] John Chipman Gray, *The Nature and Sources of the Law,* 2d Ed. 38-39 (New York: The MacMillan Company 1921). (Footnote omitted.)

birth out of wedlock is not uncommon. In this climate, the stigma for illegitimacy is not as pronounced as formerly. To its credit the Supreme Court has been instrumental in mandating equal treatment at law for the illegitimate child. We have stated and rephrased the question numerous times. Indulge us once more. Is there something about law in the abstract that prevents the unborn from having rights? Some years ago prior to the emotional demand for abortion surfaced, John Chipman Gray, a leading writer of jurisprudence, stated in a matter-of-fact fashion: "Has a child begotten, but not born, rights? There is no difficulty in giving them to it." Mr. Gray, of course, died without having a chance to peruse the *Wade* decision and find out that there was difficulty. The entire passage from Gray follows as well as a part of an interesting footnote to the same source. Included in human beings, normal and abnormal, as legal persons, are all living beings having a human form. But they must be *living* beings; corpses have no legal rights. Has a child begotten, but not born, rights? There is no difficulty in giving them to it. A child, five minutes before it is born, has as much real will as a child five minutes after it is born; that is, none at all. It is just as easy to attribute the will of a guardian, tutor, or curator to the one as to the other. Whether this attribution should be allowed, or whether the embryo should be denied the exercise of legal rights, is a matter which each legal system must settle for itself. In neither the Roman nor the Common Law can a child in the womb exercise any legal rights. But putting an end to the life of an unborn child is generally in this country an offense by statute against the State; and in our Law a child once born is considered for many purposes as having been alive from the time it was begotten.'[70]

Footnote 2 to this passage reads in part:

The history of the development of the Common Law on this subject is curious. Originally, a child does not seem to have been considered for any purpose as living before his birth. The House of Lords, at the end of the seventeenth century, misunderstanding the existing law, and to the great disgust of the Judges, allowed a child who was begotten but not born at the end of a life estate to take the property as if he had been born

---

[70]   /*Id.* at 39.

at that date. Then the doctrine was extended to cover all cases where it was for the benefit of the child to be considered as having been born.[71]

The first time someone set about granting the unborn rights, it was to "the great disgust of the Judges." Did history repeat itself in 1973 when Texas' life rights were taken away? The "difficulty" with *Wade* was that the American Bar Association, the American Medical Association, Planned Parenthood, the American Civil Liberties Union, and others-mega-goliath- ganged up on the poor, defenseless—in more ways than one—unborn undavid. Surely, these prestigious organizations would not lead us astray! When one has capitulated lock, stock and barrel to the pro-abortion schematic, one can easily write off the anti-abortion argument, one in which the only' ones fostering the unborn's side are various right to life organizations. The Court did not say so in *Wade*, but part of the pro-abortion argument is that the anti-abortion statutes are directly linked with religion, more specifically, the Roman Catholic Church. The State of Texas was not allowed to adopt one theory of life according to the Court. But Texas did so a century ago—and all without the help of religion. It was that pro-abortion mentality that condemns the theory of life, and nothing else. Aristotle posited his three-stage theory of life before Christianity was founded. Surely the legislature had the right to modify this thinking when physicians were demanding this be done.

Does a child begotten but not born have rights? A simple question, raised by the noted writer of jurisprudence, John Chipman Gray. His own answer: "There is no difficulty in giving them to it." So why did the *Wade* Court run into such a stumbling block? Why didn't the Court recognize what *all* the writers of jurisprudence—the writers of judicial philosophy, if you will—have, that it is simply *not difficult* to attribute rights to the unbom.[72]

We have mentioned the creative "person in the whole sense," a phrase whose meaning, if known is known to Justice Blackmun alone. It is not a retrieval from the law of torts, property, criminal law or any other area. "Potential" is similarly an exercise in creativity when applied to the unborn. Like Alice in Wonderland, the words mean what Justice

---

[71] /*Id*. at 39.

[72] Berna rd N. Nathanson. *77le Abortion Papers* 1 77 (New York: Frederick Fell Publishers, Inc. 1983).

Blackmun chooses to have them mean. Science does not apply "potential" to the human being, law does not do so. Why does Justice Blackmun?

In Part I, we have concluded that the Supreme Court's study of history was feeble, one sided and ultimately wrong. We also mentioned our chagrin at the Court's failure to intellectually discuss—to define—the Fourteenth Amendment person. We have under taken that task in this Part. By ignoring the philosophers and theologians and by concentrating on the source that everyone should use if they are unclear on meaning, we are able to ascertain several definitions that give rise to the recognition of the unborn as a person. At that point, we can readily associate the unborn with the legal person and yes, the constitutional person.

Locke has told us that government has no end but the preservation of life, liberty and property. We used to hear on television: "Is it life or is it Memorex?" In its own way, the Court selected Memorex for the unborn. In doing so, in the manner in which it did, the Court violated Locke's first rule, for it frustrated the goal that government *had no other end* but to preserve, first and foremost, life. The amazing postscript is that years have followed, and the Court has not budged from its error.

Was the Supreme Court wrong in *Wade?* While we are inclined to say they were wrong in the whole sense, we know that answer will not do. *Wade* was wrong in not providing representation for the unborn. Wrong in its presentation of history. Wrong in not asking whether Texas' ·life was Fourteenth Amendment life. Wrong in not defining person. Wrong in excluding the unborn from the dictionary meaning of person. Wrong in not searching out and applying the dictionary meaning of person. Wrong in not recognizing that scientifically, the unborn was a human being from conception. Wrong in not adjudicating with traditional evidence the status of the unborn.

We have raised the issues of: (1) whether the unborn constitutes life under state law; (2) whether the unborn constitutes life under the Fourteenth Amendment; (3) whether the unborn is a person under state law, and (4) whether the unborn is a person within the meaning of the Fourteenth Amendment. The answers are yes, four times over.

THEORY OF LIFE

The Supreme Court denounced Texas for adopting a theory of life. This was another error of the Court. The physicians did adopt such a theory and this was passed on to the state legislatures. The physicians of the Nineteenth Century exercised excellent judgement in reaching their conclusions without the aid of the philosophers and theologians. *Wade* would have us believe these physicians were wrong. Seemingly at some point, the Court will be embarrassed by at least one of its many errors in *Wade*. We would suggest that this is the most embarrassing of all. For it is a simple matter to ascertain that a physician should reach a medical judgement based upon the best knowledge that science has to offer at the time. The Court more than a century later says the physicians and legislatures must only adopt a theory that meets with the approval of philosophers and theologians—present and past. We have not read every case that the Supreme Court has handed down, but we are willing to make a small wager that *Wade's* nonsense about the lack of doctor philosopher-theologian consensus coupled with the prohibition of Texas "adopting on theory of life" must be the all-time most absurd observation by the Supreme Court. Obviously, the writer of *Wade* was bewitched by the women's liberation movement. It is possible for a substantial number of expert physicians to readopt this same theory of life. Under the *Wade* approach, the physician must not only be a scientist but must keep in touch with all the philosophers of the world, past and present, and the religions—at least Christian and Jewish. Our Twentieth Century physicians do not seem to be cognizant of this, but the Court has belittled the efforts of their Nineteenth Century counterparts and has attempted to advise them that they should not do likewise in this century. Thus, when we ask whether the unborn constituted life under state law, our answer must be yes. On the Texas law books for approximately a century, the Texas abortion statute reflects a theory of life gained from the physician's knowledge and experience. We simply cannot accept the Court's statement that Texas may not adopt that theory of life. If such is the case, it means that all scientific facts and theories, before being sent to a legislature for consideration in enacting a law, must first be given the acid test, the scrutinization by the many philosophers and theologians. It necessarily follows from *Wade* that scientific fact will not be accepted as such by the Supreme Court unless the fact is first verified and is approved by a consensus of philosophers and theologians. The unborn child, because unwanted, is punished for this status of unwantedness by being aborted, or in the words of the Texas statute, by being destroyed. One cannot help but recall the forceful words of Justice Brennan in his concurring opinion in *Furman v. Georgia:* The true significance of these punishments is that they treat members of the human race as nonhumans, as objects to be toyed with and discarded.[73]

While Brennan was speaking of capital punishment, the words have the additional advantage of describing the abortion deaths to a "T." What is distressing is that he did not make that connection when he voted in *Wade* less than a year later.

CONCLUSION

Science does not recognize potential human beings, potential animals, or potential plants, we believe. It deals with the real thing. "Potential," while found in the dictionary, was not applied to human being prior to *Wade* and several other abortion courts. While it may be a philosophic term, it is not commonly employed by scientists. Similarly, person in the whole sense does not make good dictionary sense, does not have a settled meaning at law, and is not employed by science. The illegitimate, the corporation, and the child already born have not been required to establish themselves as such. Singling out the unborn child appears to be yet another example of bias. The more one scrutinizes "person in the whole sense," the more one realizes that it is not more than high-sounding nonsense. It is time for the real expert to stand up and be counted, the physician or other scientist who concerns himself or herself with the question of the scientific status of the unborn. Other physicians are not necessary. At the same time, the lawyers, the philosophers and theologians should be ignored as to their view or position. It cannot be emphasized too much that as in other questions of medicine, a scientific solution is called for.

The main part of any abortion case should be the probing of medical experts. Either they will or will not establish the unborn as a human being. This is to be done in court proceedings with cross-examination

---

[73]   408 u.s. 238. 72-73 (1972).

made possible. Only then should the evidence be weighed and evaluated. In the *Wade* opinion, we find no indication that the testimony · of a single physician was submitted and considered. Under these circumstances, it is premature and prejudicial to assume what the evidence will be, as to which the *Wade* Court · can be justly criticised.

Expert witnesses must be divided between the dead and the living. The dead, of course, are unable to be resurrected to testify; they cannot be cross-examined. We must rely on their written record. The living, to qualify as an expert, must be subjected to the process of cross-examination. In its muddled thinking, the Court failed to distinguish as to living and dead. The advocate of the unborn must insure that this not happen again.

Cross-examination is the bulwark of the unborn. Because we do not believe that the theologians and philosophers will be sustained under close scrutiny, we are recommending against the unborn's advocate calling them. We believe a court would be in error accepting expert testimony from a theologian as it would taint the case with religion. In a nation that lives by the separation of church and state, it makes no sense to project a theologian as an expert.

Additionally, as there are more than 3000 Christian sects in the United States, it would appear that if one can be heard, so can another. The Jews would have to be accepted. Would Moslems and others not of the Judeo-Christian ethic? When it comes to abortion, there should be no religious favorites. One religion is as good as another—totally unnecessary.

With the philosophers, one runs into the problem of different schools or systems of thought. Which school does one select? The answer: none. "The Fourteenth Amendment does not enact Mr. Herbert Spencer's Social Statics... but a Constitution is not intended to embody a particular economic theory, whether of paternalism and the organic relations of the citizen to the State or of *laissez faire.* "[74]

In any event, let the opposition claim the philosophers and theologians as their own. Cross-examine vigorously. Can we bury the concept of "consensus" once and for all? It seems that if consensus were the standard—and *Wade* indicated it is so—we would have lost

---

[74]   *Lochner v. New York*. 198 U.S. 45. 75 (1905) (Holmes, concurring).

the benefit of what Einstein had to offer, for his theories were hardly a consensus of other views. The crucial question does not lead one to take a count and see how many agree. The most important point, which was lost in the *Wade* confusion, is what is or seems to be right. Yes, "consensus" should be replaced effectively by "rightness."

We dissent from the Court's apparent position that the American Bar Association and the American Public Health Association are experts in the area of abortion. These nameless, faceless organizations are representative bodies, not persons or human beings, who can be cross-examined. For the same reason, the American Medical Association is not an expert, but from its ranks, we can find experts. We believe it is misleading to characterize all physicians as experts on the status of the unborn, as we believe many have not kept up with the literature and that some have little interest in the subject. Under these circumstances, it is not right to make the blanket statement that the doctors are the experts.

As we bid our final adieu to the philosophers and theologians in this Part, we are mindful of Justice Blackmun's words that Texas may not adopt one theory of life. When that "theory" was proposed by the medical profession in the last century, it was at a time when there was consensus in the medical community. Throwing out the philosophers and theologians, it is only logical and responsible to heed the call of the physicians. Ultimately, if the medical profession promulgates a theory of life, the legislature not only has the right but the responsibility to embrace the theory. *Wade* was wrong again, we believe, for stating otherwise. Does it make sense to in one breath recognize the unborn as an embryo and foetus and in the next breath relegate the status of the unborn as a mere *theory* of life? Without elaboration, the inconsistency is apparent.

PART III

THE 30 ERRORS OF WADE

At this point, we believe a recapitulation is in order to make it absolutely clear what our position is. As we have concentrated on the errors of *Roe v. Wade*, we intend to zero in on the major errors at this time. By major, we believe that the error of fact or law or both was of such magnitude that the unborn should be entitled to a new hearing on that basis alone.

It is common to denominate judicial errors as mistakes of fact or mistakes of law, and we will do so here.

1. *A non-party, no representation.* Someone should have alerted the trial court that it was running roughshod over the rights of the unborn. Had this been done, some of the later mistakes in the litigation might have been forestalled. We use "might" advisedly, as we believe that the emotions were so strong that even a guardian-ad-litem or other representative only might have averted the disaster. Other than abortion cases, we could find no comparable case of record where such an indispensable party was missing from the lawsuit. We believe that a trial court, spotting this error which appears plainly of record, could safely ignore *Wade* and re-adjudicate the entire constitutional dispute. An error of procedure, it rises to the level of constitutional law.

2. *Bias.* The unborn never had a chance given Justice Blackmun's out-and-out showing of favoritism for the pregnant woman. He did not raise pointed, pertinent questions: Is this a being? Does abortion result in the death of a being? What kind? Does not abortion destroy life and limb?

67

Bias is a question of judicial ethics. A court is required to give a full and fair hearing to all interested parties.

3. *History.* The common law protected the unborn after quickening, which fact was denied in *Wade.* While this error was important, we cannot categorize it as major. Even more important, which again the Court failed to find, the purpose of all those Nineteenth Century laws - one of which the *Wade* Court confronted - was to protect the life of the unborn. The purpose of these old abortion laws was the second most important fact of the case, taking a back seat only to the humanity status of the unborn. More and stronger evidence on behalf of the unborn was submitted to the American people five years later. The Court simply erred on a crucial question of fact.

4. *Fourteenth Amendment person.* In denying the unborn status as a Fourteenth Amendment person, the Court failed to define what such a person was. If we do not know what a Fourteenth Amendment person is, we have no basis to assess whether the unborn qualifies. We are convinced that along with the non-representation, the bias, the faulty history and the lack of definition of the Fourteenth Amendment, no one on the Court gave serious consideration to the inclusion of the unborn as meriting legal and constitutional protection. This is a mistake of constitutional law.

5. *Life greater than liberty.* The Court seized on liberty as the dominant value, created a strong impenetrable emotional barrier and concluded that potential life was not forceful enough to pierce the shell. Life comes first in the Constitution and is the superior value, until *Wade,* that is. The concurring justices exhibited this same misapplication. This is another mistake of constitutional law.

6. *The American Bar Association and The American Public Health Association as experts.* Whether these are experts in the Court's view or whether their voting on abortion is believed by the Court to be a significant act is not altogether clear. In either event, the Court has fallen into error. The votes of these organizations, or representatives thereof, are irrelevant to the situation of Jane Roe and her unborn child. Their inclusion was prejudicial to the unborn's cause. At every turn, it seems,

bias raises its ugly head. This question of the acceptability and reliability of experts is a mistake of evidence or fact.

7. American Medical Association as experts. Our inclination is to state that the AMA of the last century, acting unopposed, were experts under the prevailing circumstances. Certainly, the AMA's votes of 1967 and 1970 cannot be deemed to be the act of an expert, given the large number of physicians, apparently, who are making no claim to be an expert. The number of actual experts is, we believe, just a fraction of the medical profession. *Wade* should have recognized the limiting value of the AMA votes in 1967 and 1970, and its prejudicial effect on the unborn. This error is a mistake of fact.

8. Physicians, philosophers and theologians. The physician is a scientist, the other two are not. With more than 3000 Christian religions in the United States, we do not know which theologians to seek out. We are surprised that Justice Blackmun did not recognize the obviously impermissible entanglement with religion that would violate the First Amendment. Or did bias once again confuse him? We do not think philosophers are qualified to give a scientific opinion. So why would we even want their opinion? Although not mentioned by the *Wade* Court, in examining the philosophers, we are likely to run into competing systems or schools with conflicting claims. As stated earlier, we do not believe that the Constitution allows for selecting one of the philosophers or schools of philosophers. But if they are to be heard, it should be in a Court of law subject to cross-examination. The error of recognizing any physician, any philosopher and any theologian as an expert is once again a mistake of fact.

9. Consensus. We do not believe that in selecting "consensus" the Supreme Court was employing the traditional standard, which is to judge experts and expert testimony by the use of cross-examination. The doctors need not all agree, as most of them are non-experts. As such, their view is unimportant. Spare us from "consensus" and decide by *judging* what is right. In the search for consensus, one takes a count; in the traditional method, the court weighs the evidence. The difference between the two is often remarkable. As we suggested earlier, weighing the facts, perhaps competing, distinguishes adjudication from debatesmanship. This error, we believe, is a mistake of law.

10. *Potential life.* We cannot be sure what Justice Blackmun really meant when he used the phrase. We believe that if he cleanses himself from the influences of the philosopher and theologian, he may begin thinking like a scientist. Is this a vegetable, an animal or a human being? We think he will find that it is one or the other, but that he will be able to discard the curious "potential." In any event, as the word "life" is crucial, we believe it was an error to describe it as "potential" without defining the term. We are not entirely sure how to categorize this error, but it seems to be a mistake of mixed law and fact.

11. *Person in the whole sense.* No matter how much we strain, we are in no position to state what a person in the whole sense is. There is no such person. This is a mistake of law.

12. *One theory of life.* The Supreme Court declared that Texas could not adopt one theory of life. Fresh on the minds of the Court was the notion that it required a consensus of the scientific, philosophical and religious thinkers. We have endeavored to show that the philosophers and theologians can be ignored. When physicians are traveling over the states proclaiming the unborn is human life, the legislators are fully empowered to adopt this theory, or fact, of life. Is it so reprehensible to place the unborn human offspring among human beings? At all times, the human unborn is a being that can only be plant, animal or human. This is not a theory of life in the sense of speculation. It is a fact of life in that science offers no alternatives. This could properly be termed a mistake of fact.

13. *Evidence.* From a review of the opinion in the district court to a review of the opinion in the Supreme Court, we find nothing to indicate that any evidence of any kind was taken through the adjudicatory process. Neither the Texas federal district court nor the United States Supreme Court relied on medical experts who were subjected to cross-examination, nor to any other witnesses, expert or not. While we complain bitterly that the unborn offered no evidence, it seems clear that no one else did either. Surely the humanity of the unborn was disputed; surely this was a factual dispute calling for evidence. Is the unborn

smitten by bias again? We believe that the Court's failure to rely upon evidence for a disputed fact was a mistake of law.

14. *Human being.* As stated early in this book, *Roe v. Wade* is significant for what it doesn't do in the text, the mention and discussion of "human being." Were the unborn's representative writing an abortion opinion the length of *Wade,* the case would be peppered with use of the term. The three-choice definition discussed in Part II would be prominent. We believe the court's disuse of human being was intentional, fully in keeping with the sentiments of the liberal abortion movement whose main theme appears to be to deny and not disprove the humanity of the unborn. In the future, if experts testify that the unborn is simply a plant, they will be asked to explain whether this plant becomes an animal first and then a human being, how the process of change works, and whether this two or three stage transition is recognized and described in the scientific treatises. The lesson we learn from *Wade* is that if we fail to ask questions, we definitely will not get any answers. In the end, the case can be memorialized as an abortion decision which the Supreme Court, apparently because of its feminist bias, would not touch the unborn human being with a ten-foot pole. The Court found it more comfortable to dabble with "potential life". But is the comfort of the Court really a consideration? Not when humanity is at stake. The failure to find the unborn a human being was a mistake of fact.

15. *Life, the cornerstone.* The alternative to *Wade* is a case in which "life" is the predominant value. In this climate, we note that "person" in the Fourteenth Amendment has been given the broadest possible meaning. We note that there is no difficulty in giving rights to the unborn. The State of Texas was told by the medical community that human life begins at conception. Little did the Texas legislators know that some futuristic court would undercut their efforts by decreeing that they acted in ignorance and error. Declared that court, the Texas legislators should have sought out the philosophers and theologians of the ages, and if they discovered disagreement, they should not only have enacted a restrictive abortion law but they should have taken the further step to abolish the prior law based on quickening. Abortion means "the life of the embryo or fetus shall be destroyed." Recognizing that inheritance rights have been granted to the unborn for more than 200 years, we put

forth the proposal that life is the most fundamental of the fundamental rights, and consequently, should be the first right. Does it do violence to and does it distort the meaning of the Fourteenth Amendment to include the unborn? Is the human unborn offspring essentially human, animal or plant? What does science tell us? We would submit that if the great concept of life is in fact and in law accorded the status of numero uno, the "theory of life" of Texas legislation coincides with the "theory of life" in the Fourteenth Amendment. Justice Blackmun stated that if the Fourteenth Amendment unborn person were established, the claim for the pregnant woman collapses. In our view, if the Fourteenth Amendment claim of life is realized, the maternal claim never gains a foothold and stagnates in a position of ruin. What do these words have in agreement: religion, speech, life and abortion? As of 1973, all are declared to be constitutional rights. Religion, speech and life share in common that they are specifically guaranteed by the Constitution. The *Wade* Court could not find privacy or abortion in the Constitution, but decided it was implied in one of two provisions. Query: Why would the Court, in an abortion case, rush to privacy, not mentioned in the Constitution, and ignore life, specifically guaranteed by the document? The only reason we can find is that the Court, misty eyed because of its tendencies toward the woman's liberation position, simply forgot. What is this life guaranteed by the Fourteenth Amendment? Does it include, for the sake of argument, potential life or potential human life? We tum to *Webster's Ninth New Collegiate Dictionary*. A glance reveals twenty separate definitions for "life." Our hopes are buoyed. Perhaps hidden in there somewhere is something that will be of benefit to the unborn. We begin at the beginning: • 'la: the quality that distinguishes a vital and functional being from a dead body."[1] Our first thoughts: all of medical science is in agreement that the unborn is a vital and functional being and not a dead body. Our second thoughts: *potential* is a misnomer; the unborn is not *potential* life, is not *possible* life, but is a living being. Regardless of how many legal writers, regardless of how many abortion cases designated the unborn as potential, it was wrong to do so unless of course, the writer had some special meaning which should have been

---

[1] By permission. From p. 689 *Webster's Ninth New Collegiate Dictionary* ©1987 by Merriam-Webster Inc., publisher of the Merriam-Webster® Dictionaries.

given. An unbiased court would have asked: *Can* the unborn constitute Fourteenth Amendment life? *Should* the unborn constitute Fourteenth Amendment life? Can and should are fair questions. In error, the Court literally skirted the issue. The meaning of life in the Fourteenth Amendment is a question of mixed fact and law which the *Wade* Court failed to address.

16. *Privacy.* Justice Blackmun: "This right of privacy ...is broad enough to encompass a woman's decision whether or not to terminate her pregnancy." The Supreme Court did not define "privacy," but did indicate it was personal. We do not believe ourselves to be out of line to ask what it means. For Jane Roe, it meant two things: (1) the right to decide whether to abort and, if she did, (2) the right to have a physician perform it. As earlier when we did not know the meaning of a word, we resort to *Webster's Ninth New Collegiate Dictionary* for definitions:

1. a: the quality or state of being apart from company or observation: SECLUSION
   b: freedom from unauthorized intrusion <one's right to - >
2. *archaic:* a place of seclusion
3. SECRECY.[2]

   Seemingly applicable to the abortion situation is "freedom from unauthorized intrusion." Thus, as we already argued earlier, it was prejudicial to the unborn to declare a woman had the right to privacy or an abortion until it was first determined whether the unborn had the right to life. Had the unborn had the right to life, the intrusion would have been unauthorized. It is not privacy until one determined that the intrusion is not warranted. In tagging abortion as privacy without first assessing the status of the unborn, the Court jumped the gun and trashed the very meaning of privacy. According to the dictionary, one does not start out with abortion being privacy. One arrives at that only after the possible intrusions have been ruled out. *Wade* ran roughshod over the dictionary, paved the way with emotionalism

---

[2]   By permission. From p. 936 *Webster's Ninth New Collegiate Dictionary* ©1987 by Merriam-Webster Inc., publisher of the Merriam-Webster«' Dictionaries.

and later held that life was not an authorized intrusion. It is one thing to use words, i.e. potential life and person in the whole sense that are lacking in clarity; it is a graver error to decimate a word that is said to be a fundamental right in the Constitution.

The Court most certainly began the constitutional discussion from a feminist's point of view claiming that abortion is a fundamental right of privacy. Thus, it is obvious that the Court prematurely and erroneously declared abortion privacy a fundamental right. With the goo goo eyes of a feminist, the Court belatedly and reluctantly touched upon the unborn. For the Court to pounce upon abortion as a fundamental right of privacy was a major error in that it violates the ordinary use of the word "privacy," and, as we have seen, was one more insurmountable biased intrusion into the rights of the unborn: the right to fair treatment. For the Court to misapply such a word in the dictionary is a wrong, in this case, a major wrong.

Had the court bothered to consult a dictionary, it may have avoided this error. Just one more example of "raw judicial power" running helter-skelter. This is a mistake of constitutional law.

17. *States rights.* The dissenting opinions would have us believe that abortion is a matter of states' rights, meaning the state should be free to adopt whatever approach to abortion that it chooses. It is our contention that as the Nineteenth Century laws bestowed the legal right to life, the logical effect is that this embraced the constitutional right to life. A legal person is a Fourteenth Amendment person. If a state modified or erased its Nineteenth Century law to the detriment of the unborn, this was unconstitutional for interfering with the life rights of a Fourteenth Amendment person. Alternatively, the unborn, not a vegetable or animal, is a human being from conception. A human being is a fourteenth amendment person who cannot be deprived of life without due process. For these reasons, we would submit that quite clearly· a state may not pass whatever abortion legislation it chooses. The life of the unborn stands in the way. This is a mistake of constitutional law.

We believe that the existence of just one of these 17 errors would be grounds to reconsider *Roe v. Wade.* But the presence of all 17 warrants a swift rescue squad. Assuming that an abortion case is filed and further assuming that the unborn loses-*Wade* has conditioned us to assume the worst- the unborn's advocate should press for an expeditious appeal. While *Wade* is a wrong that should be righted, due to the gravity of the ever continuing loss of life, it is a wrong that should be rushed into oblivion. In fairness, we would like to point out the good features of *Roe v. Wade*. But in all honesty, there is nothing in the case which commands our praise. With the case exhibiting 17 major errors, we believe the fate of the case is sealed. What can you say about a court that excluded the unborn from participation and failed to define the fourteenth amendment person?

A lot of hoopla has surrounded the question of abortion, and we are told how complicated and complex the issues are. But we believe that we have reached the point where goodbye to population growth, pollution, poverty and racial overtones-abortion, with all the emotional baggage stripped away, presents but one single fact at issue, the status of the unborn. Recalling that *Roe v. Wade* took no real evidence on this issue is appalling. Its paper analysis was inconclusive: woe is me, the experts fail to agree, therefore i am in no position to move forward, reasoned the court. Despite indicating that the court was giving up because there was no consensus, the *Wade* court took a contrary approach, assuming that it had been proved that the unborn was non-human. Thus, it held that texas was without authority to adopt a theory of life. We would expect that the court would say we do not know what is correct at this point in the development of man's knowledge, so we have no intellectual basis for determining that your theory of life is wrong. The court, if aware of its own limitations, would not have adopted its own theory of non-life during the first two or three trimesters of fetal life. The Court's love affair with privacy was unbridled. It neglected to respect life or "possible" life of the unborn. It neglected to recognize Texas' right to deal with an issue as the State thought best in an area where even the Supreme Court admitted its confusion. While the philosophers, theologians and physicians most definitely failed to prove that the unborn was not human, the Court, in willy-nilly fashion, acted as if the point had been proven beyond all doubt.

While the Court admitted in effect its own incompetency, it set about to issue a decree disproving it. For a decision that is too flaked with uncertainty, the Court, in invalidating all the abortion laws in all the states, proceeded with an air that it was cocksure of itself. Perhaps the final chapter, on the decision will be: And so it came to pass that *Roe v.*

Wade, noxious and obnoxious in the whole sense, was aborted at mid-life and collapsed.

The Court paid as much attention to philosophers and theologians as it does medical doctors. The ladies and gentlemen of modern medical science have yet to take a stand on the 'status of the unborn. Their solution of the early 1970's was easy and convenient for them. They dodged the central issue. Thus for example, the eight week old fetus - or is it an embryo or something else - is either a human being or it is not. Can these scientists treat something that they are not sure exists? Do they ever call in the botanist or horticulturalist to treat the unborn? Do they call for a veterinarian? If not, do they have any way of determining whether the unborn is human? at is the purpose and function of the American Medical Association? If the organization is unable to face what the Association in its embryonic stage confronted, does it have any value other than of a professional social club? If there exists the inability to provide a definitive statement on the status of the unborn, what should we make of the purported professional ethics? If they cannot figure out whether they are dealing with a human being or not, how can they possibly know whether their set of ethical standards are right or not? We are curious whether the medical profession took the suggestion of Justice Blackmun to heart and scrapped the Hippocratic Oath as it pertained to abortion. If this was done, was it because the physicians were influenced by Blackmun's words and the *Wade* decision as a whole, or was it because the profession after more than 2,000 years ascertained that Hippocrates was wrong? Does some of the profession continue to cling to the Oath in its original version? If there is a split, which side is right? Both cannot be.

We believe that inviting the medical profession to tell us how many forms of life they recognize and by asking them where the unborn fits in, we might lay a basis for arriving at a solution within the medical community. At this point when we are addressing the medical community, we no longer mean the physicians as a whole. Rather, we mean the few who are the real experts. Not everyone claiming to be one will necessarily be one. The expert will have a sharp scientific mind capable of understanding the data as a scientist. Such an individual should be able to reach a conclusion not premised on what other colleagues may think or the population in general believes. Despite *Roe v. Wade,* the expert will do without philosophers and theologians. If the AMA is in charge of ethics, we recommend that body waste no time. One closing thought on ethics: If the neurosurgeons had a particular difficulty, they are not likely to call in the profession as a whole for a solution. Why not the same approach for abortion? As one Council Bluffs physician queried, does performing an abortion make one an expert?' We would suggest not because such a one is not necessarily a scientific mind.

One may ask whether my explanation of 17 major errors was oversale on my part We've reviewed them as late as May 1999, and conclude that all are valid complaints. We wrote Parts I, II, and ill, and then decided to count and describe them in part IV. In preparation for a third lawsuit in Thurston County, NE, which I filed in December of 1999, I had to proceed pro se as I could not find an attorney who would take the case. As you can see, I've uncovered 13 additional errors as of year 2000.

Error 18 Procedural Due Process As we will now reveal, we made several errors of omission. Every abortion in the country violates procedural due process: the life taken without a hearing. While we complained about this with respect to Jane Roe's baby, we omitted this multiple repetition in all abortion matters. Of the 35 or 40 million unborn children who have been killed. I don't know if a single one of them were represented in court. This is a mistake of law.

Error 19 Equal Protection Various arguments could be formulated for equal protection, e.g., the unborn child is just as much a person as a wanted unborn child just as much a person as his father and mother, just as much as every born child. In fact the unborn has a greater need for legal protection when his mother doesn't want him. Equal protection should mean that every pregnant woman must seek prenatal medical care. This is a mistake of law.

Error 20 Life Should be Given a Broad Meaning I neglected to recite that words in a constitution should be given a broad interpretation to achieve its purpose. When Justice Blackmun started out with privacy, not even in the Constitution, he effectively smothered out life. As I have noted in our brief to be submitted for another round of judicial battles, life is the key word in the Constitution. It is the dominant concept. Like a magnet, it is the controlling force in the 14th Amendment. The validity of abortion rest on how "life" related to "person", "due process" and "equal protection". Consequently, on speaks of due process and life and so on.

We do not think that in a fresh presentation to the Court, silence can remain on these issues. The unborn is incensed with *Wade* and *Casey* for not addressing the 14th Amendment on life!

This is a mistake of mixed fact and law.

Error 21 Immorality Since I conclude that the unborn is a human being, it does not follow that matters of morality should be turned over to the churches. Morality as defined in the dictionary does not depend upon religious values. Thus, the justices should have pursued the issue as a constitutional issue inquiring into the meaning of moral and proceeded from there.

This is a mistake of law.

Error 22 To Murder Abortion is the murder of the unborn child. It should carry the same penalty as the first degree murder for any abortionist Since a child is a born or unborn person, it follows that they are equal. We go further and state that the newly born child is equal for purposes of life--to his mother, father or any other person. Equal protection makes it so. Also, equal protection requires that the penalty for interrupting the life of the unborn and born should be the same: hence, when it is intentional, capital punishment is in order.

This is a mistake of law.

Error 23 A Matter of Trust There exists a unique relationship between a mother and her unborn child. There is a special bond. The woman, even though she does not want the child, must nourish it. It is an independent being but totally dependent on her for life and health. But no one seems to talk about this. She has the power but not the right to do it.

This is a mistake of law.

Error 24 An Abuse of Power in *Roe v Wade*. It trampled on the rights of the unborn at every step of the way. Justice White called this "raw judicial power". A, case can be made that he, Justice Blackmun could be removed from office. But it is too late, as Justice Blackmun has died. Judges who blindly follow *Wade* and who refuse to listen to the unborn's side should be driven from office.

Read all the Supreme Court and Federal Courts decisions on abortions beginning with *Wade* and you will discover that there exists thousands of pages of bullshit because the unborn didn't get to participate so it is not binding on the new crop of unborn. And to me arguing on behalf of the unborn, it is not based on the genuine principle, that the right to life should have governed all subsequent abortion.

Further that at the turn of the century (1901) Texas life would have been 14th Amendment life. And the Wisconsin human being would have been a 14th Amendment person. But the "biased jurist" exercised his silence in 1973.

This is a mistake of law.

Error 25 The Perpetuation of Stupidity The federal judiciary has been bombarded with abortion cases since *Wade* wasting valuable time and expense and still not figuring out that the unborn is the central figure in any abortion. An unprincipled decision leads to much stupidity when you try to apply it. On the other hand, had the court centered in on the right to life, all of this foolishness could have been avoided.

This is a mistake of mixed fact and law.

Error 26 Life is the Most Fundamental Right Who would argue that speech or religion is greater than life? Without life none of the others exist. Hopefully in the future the Supreme Court will announce that the right to life is the most fundamental of the fundamental rights. When life is in issue it should be the first order of business.

This is a mistake of law.

Error 27 Thou Shall Not Kill Even though this is found in the bible it is a valuable principle just as thou shall not steal. In a Christian-Jewish nation the principle exist in every jurisdiction what religion could possibly object? What other would object? Every act of abortion is a killing act.

Has the Supreme Court ever mentioned this? Could it be biased? The un-represented unborn is waiting for some court to talk about killing and murder. Some justices have, recently in dissent.

This is a mistake of mixed fact and law.

Error 28 The Definition of child-bearing Of or relating to the process of conceiving, being pregnant with, and giving birth to children," *Merriam Webster's Collegiate Dictionary lOth Ed. 198.* This should be the irrefutable clincher to Justice Blackmun and Justice O'Connor the child exists at conception.

In *Roe v Wade The* Court didn't use the dictionary, remarkably, in *United States v. Vuitch* 402 U.S. 62 (1971). The court relied on Webster's Dictionary to resolve an abortion case. The decision was somewhat of a victory for the feminist movement To Justice O'Connor the child exists at viability.

This is a mistake of fact.

Error 29 The Definition of "Child" Blackmun used the word which Planned Parenthood seems to dread. As it is a recently born or unborn person, the word merited a call.

This is a mistake of fact.

Error 30 A Crooked Justice A bird's eye view of why Wade is bad law and why Justice Blackmun was crooked and corrupt.

This is a judicial abuse of power, so an abuse of law.

PART IV

THE MEDICAL PROFESSION

MY ONE-WAY VISIT WITH THE MEDICAL ORGANIZATIONS

The AMA and state medical societies and associations must share in the blame. How could they possibly allow for abortions even if the state law called for it? It was tantamount to saying that murder was all right if authorized by law. Surely some of the State ethical committees would and should have made liberal abortion unethical in their state. In the early 90's we sent a five-page cover letter to the AMA ethical committee and an identical copy to all the states medical societies and associations. Not a single one was returned to me, so I have to assume they were delivered and received.

The jist of the letter was that the medical ethics committees were wrong on abortion --at least that was my hope to convince them. Even though I write on behalf of not yet born, I am not affiliated with any right to life organization.

I am aware that some medical societies and associations have simply relied on the AMA's ethics. But if you are a state ethics committee member, I would suggest that the ultimate responsibility for your state rests with you. This is being sent to committee chairman and I would ask that you send a copy to each committee member in your state, even if you disagree with what I say.

As I will point out to you shortly, the 19th century medical profession led the battle to have restrictive abortion laws. As we are nearing the end of the 20th century, I am challenging the medical community to similarly take over the leadership.   ·

Planned Parenthood was opposed to abortion, and the ACLU had taken no stand.

If abortion were truly a right of constitutional magnitude, the proposition should have been raised in the courts then—and earlier. But the fact remains that of all the reported abortion decisions from that time frame, defense attorneys simply did not routinely raise the issue. We are confident that, in 1953, for example, the unborn would have been afforded the right to live with little opposition, which was the case by virtue of state law.

We suspect the unborn would not have been elevated to the status of Fourteenth Amendment person. Rather, the rationale that the unborn was deserving of protection by the state would have been linked to the state public policy as the dissenters in *Wade* suggested. The feminist claim of the outright justice of abortion on demand created the need for opposition, and the right to life organizations were formed. Emotionalism awoke. Thus, we urge on the Court to hold at bay the emotional appeals of the five years preceding *Wade* and re-think the entire matter of abortion from the vantage point of the golden age of the fifties.

April 1991

To: Members of Medical Ethics Committees

From: Daniel McTaggart, Author of *Abortion and the Outlaw*, the first and only book to fully analyze *Roe vs. Wade*

RE: Medical Ethics and Abortion

PREFACE

I have spent 20 years working on the problem of abortion. I began before *Roe v. Wade* was decided. I believe that I've mastered *Wade* in the sense that I understand the case fully. I don't know who else can make that claim.

In this memo I am going to try to convince you that medical ethics is wrong on abortion. Lest you think I am unfairly targeting physicians, my book is claiming that the Supreme Court made 17 major errors in *Wade*.

THE SUPREME COURT ON PHYSICIANS

I assume that very few have read the case so I begin by summarizing what it said concerning physicians.

In 1859 and 1871 the AMA determined that the unborn constituted human life from conception. Was this a correct determination?

In 1970 the Judicial Council handed down an ethical opinion that abortion was all right if it didn't "violate the laws of the community, following the lead of the House of Delegates."

The ethics opinion did not state whether the unborn constituted human life. Does it? How can an ethical opinion be drawn if you don't know whether the unborn is human life. Was the AMA wrong in 1871? If not, they were right. I would suggest that the medical profession has the obligation to resolve this issue. In 1971, approximately 12 states had liberal abortion laws. The rest were restrictive.

The Court stated that the real reason for the 19th century restricted laws was maternal health and that it was "sharply disputed" whether the purpose of the laws was to protect the unborn.

Wade was decided in 1973. In 1968 a book was published by historian James C. Mohr which showed that state by state physicians went to their legislators to lobby for a bill to protect the unborn. As far as I can tell the Supreme Court still has not acknowledged its error in downplaying the status of the unborn in 1973. Once again the question naturally arises: Did the physicians in the states err in the 19th century when they argued successfully for the protection of the unborn? *Wade:* "We need not resolve the difficult question of when life begins. When those trained in the respective disciplines of medicine, philosophy and theology are unable to arrive at any consensus, the judiciary, at this point in the development of a man's knowledge, is not in a position to speculate as to answer."

I believe that the Supreme Court insulted the physicians. They are scientists: the other two are not. The philosophers and theologians in the 19th century did not object, nor did they provide much assistance, when the physicians went around the country gaining protection for the unborn. *Wade* is a curious case in that the court had no evidence before it. Not a single physician was put under oath. Do physicians in their daily work commonly seek the guidance of philosophers and (theologians?) By being placed on the same level as the philosophers and theologians, the physicians have been insulted. Were the physicians in 1970 acting as good scientists or were they merely bowing to the pressure of the feminist movement?

Is THE UNBORN HUMAN?

1. Adult. Can you define or describe the adult human being in such a manner that a general consensus would agree with you? It's never been done.
2. Unborn. It follows that if you ask whether and when the unborn is a human being you will not reach a consensus. One might say that it becomes human when the heart develops sufficiently; right to lifers argued before the Supreme Court that once conceived by human parents, you are human. Of course, everyone doesn't agree.
3. Child. Twice in *Doe vs. Bolton*, a companion case to *Roe v. Wade*, the Court used the term "unborn child." *Webster's Ninth New Collegiate Dictionary*, defines child as an unborn or recently born person." The the court in *Bolton* unwittingly admitted that the unborn was a person.
4. Aristotle was, among other things, a scientist. He believed the unborn was first a vegetable, then an animal, and then become a human. Scientist still rely on these three categories, but I bet that they can't call the unborn a vegetable: if so, which one; nor an animal: if so, which one? You, as scientist, have no other categories for living things, so today which is the logical category that the human unborn would fit into? I suggest you check a biology book used at the high school or college level. How would they treat the unborn? Dear medical scientist, how are you going to get the right answer if you don't ask the right question?
5. Person. In the big, fat dictionaries you found in the library person is defined as "a human being as opposed to an animal or thing." Not all desk copies of the dictionary contain this definition. But obviously it is a reversal of Aristotelian view mentioned in the preceding section.
6. Patient. I believe the medical profession uses this word in the Oath. Obviously at times there are more than one patient. I saw

on TV a few nights ago that it is now very safe to give blood transfusions to fetuses. How can one be a patient in one doctor's office and something to disregard in another?

7. Inferior Human Beings. Before the civil War, blacks were looked on by many as inferior human beings. Call the developing unborn inferior if you will, but also call it a human being. Society must protect the inferior more than those who are not. Are the medical scientist ready to protect the inferior Unborn?

8. Potential Human Being is a phrase used by the Supreme Court to describe the unborn. This seems to be erroneous scientifically as we discussed above. If the unborn were an animal or plant at some time it would be a potential human being.

9. Human Life. As was stated earlier, the 1859 and 1871 AMA conclusions were that the unborn constituted human life. Have you proved them wrong?

CONCLUSION

It seems to me that the ordinary and thoughtful person (being neither pro-life nor pro choice) would readily conclude that it is alright to consider the unborn as a child, a person, a human being. How about the ordinary and thoughtful doctor? I don't think that important, intelligent decisions should be made at conventions like the AMA's House of Delegates did in 1970. Would you like your life to hinge on the whims of a group that is more inclined to having a good time as opposed to being under oath?

ARE THERE SOME PHYSICIANS WHO ARE NOT EXPERTS ON ABORTION?

In April, 1987, I took a survey of Council Bluffs, Iowa, physicians. Of the 90 contacted, 28 responded. They were divided as to what the best abortion policy would be.

The most significant aspect of the poll was that only four considered themselves experts on abortion. All four were pro-life. This led me to believe that there were many non-experts at the AMA meeting in 1970.

The question also arises as to whether medical ethics committee members are experts on abortion. If not, shouldn't they seek out someone who is? If you had an issue respecting heart surgery, would the ethical decision be made at an AMA House of Delegates meeting? Would you consult experts?

IN CLOSING

Ethics is a matter of right or wrong. If you are on the medical ethics committee of your state, you have the solemn obligation to see that all of your decisions are correct.

Not one of those professional committees responded. I was chagrined to receive no reply, but it did fortify my belief I was right. It has been my experience that when one approach is an entity and is wrong, the entity will point out the error. When you're right they'll stonewall you.

This just seemed to strengthen my conviction that the ethics committees were themselves being unethical (even if they were relying on the AMA) because each state should have had to establish for itself what ethical opinions would govern the state. While they were acting unethically in my opinion, each time an abortion occurred is a matter of malpractice.

On February 18,1999, I sent a copy of that letter to Planned Parenthood of Sioux City and the physician who performs abortions there, as well as to Dr. Winston Crabb and Planned Parenthood of Lincoln, asking for a response by March 1, 1999. I received no reply from any of them.

Planned Parenthood v. *Casey.* had, we believe, an ethical obligation to point out that "child" is an acceptable word to use for the unborn, and that child is an unborn person.

The American Civil Liberties Union does not seem to realize that life is greater than liberty.

The states' attorneys general seem to share in the burden of distributing blame, for they should protect all persons within their jurisdiction.

All those pro-lifers who are out there praying are also to blame, for God does not want them to engage in public prayer as is explained in the series of books I'm writing called THE THIRD TESTAMENT.

SURVEY OF PHYSICIANS
Directions: Answer each Section

Section I.

An expert Is someone who·can appear in court and testify, ba!ed upon training, experience and reading the relevant literature on the subject.

_____ I am an expert on the issue of the status of the unborn a! it pertains to abortion.
_____ I am not an expert on the unborn.

Section II

Aristotle wrote that the human unborn started out a! a vegetable, changed to an animal and then to a human. Some dictionaries defme as "person" a human being as opposed to an animal or thing. Biology books are generally divided into plants (or vegetables), animals and human beings.

_____ I believe that the unborn is a human being from conception.
_____ I believe that the unborn is a vegetable for ___ weeks of gestation
_____ The unborn is this type of vegetable: _____
_____ I believe that the unborn is an animal for _____ weeks of gestation.
_____ The unborn is this type of animal: _____

Section III
Opinions vary as to when abortion should be allowed.

_____Only to protect the life of the mothers.
_____If the mother has been a victim of rape or Incest.
_____If the child may be born severely defective.
_____At any time up to ____weeks of gestation.

Explain your answer in this Section, keeping in mind the Issues when the unborn can be considered a human being.

_____

_____

Section IV

_____

_____

SECOND SURVEY OF PHYSICIANS

In April, 1992, I prepared a second survey of physicians, this time using the Omaha, Lincoln, and Norfolk, Nebraska phone books. This questionnaire was similar to the Council Bluffs survey retaining the identification by the physician of expert or non expert. Unlike the first survey, it was the request that the physician supply his or her name and address. All who responded included these identification features except one. Sixty-nine out of 429 responded. Fifteen asserted that they were experts. Sixty-five of these listed the unborn as human being from conception. That left but four to carry the day for the other side. None of these four calling themselves asserted status of an expert. In claiming to be an expert, 15 respondents maintained that the unborn is human being from conception. Nine of those calling themselves experts asserted status of an expert would allow for abortions to save the life of the mother. Four stated that the threat to life was rare. Four would never allow for abortion. Two of the self-proclaimed experts would permit abortion if the unborn was seriously defective. One would allow it if the mother had been a victim of rape or incest, as well as if it were to be known to be an AIDS baby and if its parents were known to have venereal disease.

The specialities of 14 identifying themselves as experts were family practice, with pediatrics, OB/GYN, general surgery and cardiology. The handwriting of the 15th physician was indecipherable.

The total of those considering the unborn to be a human being from conception was 61 of the 65 (including the 15 experts). The non-experts tended to be more opinionated and wordy.

But since they were not asserting that they are experts, it would serve no purpose here to explore their ideas.

We have 15% of the Council Bluffs physicians and 21% of those in the Omaha-Lincoln Norfolk area moving to the fore stating they possess the expertise to successfully topple the position taken by the Supreme Court. Forty-six percent of the Council Bluffs physicians have taken a pro-life position while a whopping 94% of the Nebraska physicians have nixed the message of *Roe v. Wade.*

The number of physicians responding in both surveys was remarkably small. We had expected much more.

We fear that some are fearful of expressing a view not wanting to alienate anyone while others not directly involved with abortion simply do not care. Most physicians, we believe, were not interested in any fashion, because the issue did not present itself in their practice.

I have not read any pre-*Wade* or post-*Wade* surveys of physicians, so I state with conviction that most doctors do not consider themselves an expert on abortion law. Thus is highly likely that the votes of the AMA of 1970 and 1971 were largely that of non-experts.

In the early 90's, I filed a lawsuit in Lincoln, NE. In this court, I was unable to establish a right for the unborn to have a guardian-ad-litem appointed. Though I was given ample opportunity to present my case, I didn't succeed: and I didn't think I made a good record for an appeal. In 1994, I thought I had learned from all my mistakes in Lincoln, so I went to Douglas County (Omaha) and flied suit in *Dan R. McTaggart v. Women's Services P.C.*

It was a nightmare. I got torpedoed by Judge Mary Likes, who had not been on the bench too long. Before ruling on the application for guardian-ad-litem. She ordered that I pay the multiple defendants' attorney fees. I asked her why. She said that only she "had done her homework".

There were three defense attorneys' fees a bit in excess of $1,000 each. Apparently, her ruling on this was based on Neb. Rev. Stat 28-824 in which the pleading was frivolous or bad faith. I still haven't figured this one out.

We didn't appeal because we didn't have enough money and we weren't satisfied with the presentation we had made. We cleaned out our savings accounts as the. defense attorneys agreed to $500 a piece in legal fees.

These experiences leave no alternative_never to file a lawsuit pro se. But the dilemma is that no attorney will take the case. They don't respond when I write to them. When I talk to them they don't want to get involved.

PART V

ON RELIGION

Religion has often been injected into the abortion dilemma. As a practical matter, religion covers the spectrum in the abortion controversy. Some religious groups will be pleased, some will be disappointed, however the dilemma is resolved. As religion possesses no special expertise needed to decide the matter in a court of law, religion need be paid no special attention. When some on one side proclaim that having an abortion is immoral and some on the other side declare that to not allow· an abortion is immoral, it becomes clear that religion is not likely to be instrumental in reaching a conclusion based upon law. Some readers may question whether this work is a veiled attempt at promoting one or more religious beliefs. We make every effort to disassociate ourselves from all formal religions. The following passage is from the book of Daniel, contained only in the Catholic bible, highlights our disenchantment with organized religion.

And Daniel was the king's guest, and was honored above all his friends.

2 Now the Babylonians had an idol called Bel: and there were spent upon him every day twelve great measures of fine flour, and forty sheep, and sixty vessels of wine.

3 The king also worshipped him, and went every day to adore him: but Daniel adored [Spoke to] God. And the king said to him: Why dost thou not adore Bel?

4 And he answered, and said to him: Because I do not worship idols made with hands, but [speak to] the living God, that created heaven and earth, and hath power over all flesh.

5 And the king said to him, Doth not Bel seem to thee to be a living god? Seest thou not how much he eateth and drinketh every day?

6 Then Daniel smiled and said: O king, be not deceived: for this is but clay within, and brass without, neither hath he eaten at any time.

7 And the king being angry called for his priests, and said to them: If you tell me not, who it is that eateth up these expenses, you shall die.

8 But if you can shew that Bel eateth these things, Daniel shall die, because he hath blasphemed against Bel. And Daniel said to the king: Be it done according to thy word.

9 Now the priests of Bel were seventy, besides their wives, and little ones, and children. And the king went with Daniel into the temple of Bel.

10 And the priests of Bel said: Behold we go out: and do thou, O king, set on the meats, and make ready the wine, and shut the door fast, and seal it with thy own ring:

11 And when thou comest in the morning, if thou findest not that Bel hath eaten up all, we will suffer death, or else Daniel that hath lied against us.

12 And they little regarded it, because they had made under the table a secret entrance, and they always came in by it, and consumed those things.

13 So it came to pass after they were gone out, the king set the meats before Bel: and Daniel commanded his servants, and they brought ashes, and he sifted them all over the temple before the king: and going forth they shut the door, and having sealed it with the king's ring, they departed.

14 But the priests went in by night, according to custom, with their wives and their children: and they ate and drank up all.

15 And the king arose early in the morning, and Daniel with him.

16 And the king said: Are the seals whole, Daniel? And he answered: They are whole, O king.

17 And as soon as had opened the door, the king looked upon the table, and cried out with a loud voice: Great art thou, O Bel, and there is not any deceit with thee.

18 And Daniel laughed: and he held the king that he should not go in: and he said: Behold the pavement, mark whose footsteps these are.

19 And the king said: I see the footsteps of men, and women, and children. And the king was angry.

20 Then he took the priests, and their wives, and their children: and they shewed him the private doors by which they came in, and consumed the things that were on the table.

21 The king therefore put them to death, and delivered Bel into the power of Daniel: who destroyed him, and his temple. As we read this parable the true representative of God will be able to identify and expose to the government any false religion. That being the case, the Judeo-Christian communities have had centuries to accomplish this feat, and yet "paganism" flourishes in the far east, to take one example. With respect to Christianity, we may ask whether the one, true God has required more than 200 sects to accomplish his purposes. We go so far as to pose this blunt question: is any sect of Christianity God's true religion? Daniel 14 haunts us: Is the God of Judaism and Christianity dead?

Our anguish in our falling out with the major religions is premised upon the fact that we are unable to distinguish between one religion and another. If a religion is not true, it must be false. Alas! No religion has demonstrated that it is grounded in truth. If Christianity is false, we would fare better worshiping a lion. Is our Interpretation of Daniel correct? It seems to make a great deal of sense that God's true representatives would be able to bring to light the imposters. We urge our readers to challenge their religious leaders with the issues we have raised. These concerns have prompted us to part company with all organized religion, perhaps permanently.

(THE NEW JERUSALEM BIBLE)

PART VI

PLANNED PARENTHOOD V. CASEY 505 U.S. 833 (1992)

In a 5-4 decision, the Court decided that *Roe v. Wade* should be upheld as there was nothing since *Wade* to change matters. A plurality substituted liberty as a basis, leaving Justice Blackmun alone to argue for privacy. With the liberty foundation, one had to demonstrate an "undue burden" to demonstrate a violation of liberty under the 14th Amendment. The privacy criteria would be a "compelling interest" The dissenters could do no better than to indicate that James C. Mohr's book, *Abortion in America.* proved that the 19th Century legislation was anti abortifacient, not asserting that the laws were to protect the life of the unborn, for if they were to preserve maternal health, they would also be anti abortifacient.

In her plurality opinion Justice O'Connor stated that the state had a legitimate interest in protecting maternal health and the life of the fetus that may become a child. 505 U.S. at 846. For her the unborn may be considered a child at viability. There is absolutely no basis for evolving from fetus to child. A fetus is a child. Both share the common failure to define terms. The unborn un-represented in both cases, perished for lack of an advocate to constantly challenge the judiciary.

Justice Blackmun's opinion made numerous references to potential life and nary a word about the human organism.

PART VII

ABORTION AND THE OUTLAW

In pondering the status of the unwanted unborn, we are reminded of the outlaw, not the one romanticized in television and movies, but the one who lived centuries ago in olden England.

The original outlaw was an outcast from society and was believed to have committed a felony. Having refused to do justice to others according to the law, he was removed from the protection of the law.[1] The enemy of the king, he could be killed with impunity one did not commit an offense by killing the king's enemy.[2] The outlaw's very life was insecure; to pursue the outlaw as though he were a wild beast was the right and duty of every law-abiding man.[3] These were in the days before we had sheriffs and deputies and procedures for dealing with the accused. From these beginnings, we have the startup of the criminal justice system.

The unwanted unborn is the updated version of the antiquated system of outlawry. Previously, the status of outlaw was earned by the commission of a felony; the unborn's offense is causing distress, being unwanted or

---

[1]   Frederick Pollock and Frederic William Maitland, - I *The History of English Law* 43 (Cambridge: At the University Press 1968).

[2]   *Id*. at 49.

[3]   *Id*. at 476, 477. The animal most associated with the outlaw was a wolf. *Id*. Vol. 2 at 449. We would suggest that those promoting the right to life and are searching for a new symbol might want to latch onto the wolf. The old symbol need not be abandoned. How about the last part of this decade being "the days of wolves and roses!"

causing the continuing stigma of unwed parenthood. Whereas in days of yore, every man had the right and responsibility to kill the outlaw, in modem America, the task is exclusively the province of the medical doctor. Oddly, the traditional guardians of life are the only ones empowered to destroy this form of life. "Outlawry was the capital punishment of a rude age."[4] Medical outlawry is the capital punishment of what some have called the most civilized nation the world has known. The earlier outlaw could perhaps hide or escape - to whom could he appeal if unjustly accused? Early outlawry was barbarity. The unborn outlaw has zero odds that he will avoid his fate; he is utter helplessness and defenselessness against the connivance of mother knows-best and doctor-does-best.[5]

Modern outlawry thrives. It no longer has to do with crime. The answer to the new riddle of the ages is "theory of life." The riddle: what is a human embryo and fetus? Nouveau outlawry plays the same linguistic games as does the Supreme Court. It was argued a few years back that abortion was a victimless crime. By the magic of raw judicial power, outlawry is now a victimless constitutional right in action, the only civilized thing to do.

Presto! A modem miracle! Killing an outlaw has changed from barbarism to civilized gentility, for *Wade* and the physicians have perfected the victimless outlaw. If there is destruction - *Wade* did not say that Texas must call this an act of destroying - it is a mere theory that is destroyed.

---

[4]   *Id.* at 451.

[5]   Unless and until there is a change on the horizon, we may ask the pregnant woman who she is going to call when she wants to rid her body of david. Outlaw-busters! By virtue of the AMA's 1970 vote and *Roe v. Wade,* the medical profession is afforded the sole power to extinguish life Texas-style, or "theory of life" *Wade-style.* We recognize that the bulk of the physicians do not do them by the very nature of their own limited practice, while others, dead set against the procedure, would refuse to perform abortions under any circumstances. Nevertheless, so long as all physicians are empowered to destroy the life of the unborn, we shall call them outlaw-busters. If some physicians bristle at this term believing it inapplicable in their own cases, they should work for change within their own bailiwick, the medical profession. How many medical doctors have protested to the AMA about the fact that the 1970 changes were apparently made by non-experts?

CHAPTER 1: Abortion Law Revisited

In *Roe v. Wade 410 U.S. 113* (1973), the lead opinion of Justice Blackmun stated that a woman had a fundamental right to an abortion because it was liberty or privacy. It was a 7-2 decision.

The Court states that this position "collapses" if the unborn is a 14th Amendment person. No case could be cited stating that the unborn was within the ambit of that amendment, nor that anywhere in the *Constitution* was it logical to apply person prenatally.

The Court went on to hold that when physicians, theologians, and philosophers were not able to reach a consensus on the issue of when life began, the Court, at this point in time, was in no position to speculate.

The Court seized on concepts that the unborn was a "potential life" and not a "person in the whole sense." Neither of which has a precise or accepted meaning.

I. A Modified Retrospective

There are three distinct proofs that the unborn is a constitutional person, existing as a person or human being from conception.

1. The unborn is human life. This was the conclusion of the American Medical Association in 1871. The Supreme Court is well aware of this in *Roe v. Wade*. While the AMA changed positions in 1967, eventually holding that the procedures could be allowed if permitted by state law in 1970 (See pg. 13-14, of this text). Obviously, the AMA members that voted were under the influence of the liberal feminist movement. Also of note, and more important, the members were obviously unaware that the definition of "embryo," long existing in *Dorland's Illustrated Medical Dictionary* defined the not-yet born as a "human organism." The Court tricked itself as, not having addressed it in 1967 or 1970, the official determination of human life has not been omitted by the AMA. If an unborn is human life in 1871, the unborn would logically be human life in 1973 and 2017-forever. Thus, just as Blackmun let this distinction slide and

the other court members must have concluded that the last word from the AMA was the best.

2. "Embryo" is a "human organism," according to the medical dictionary referred to above. As Justice Blackmun specifically referred to the definition without providing it, he made himself out to be liar as he stated that *potential* life, a term without clear meaning was the best he could do. The current edition of Dorland's [32nd, 2012] states that an embryo is a human organism from fertilization until the eighth week of development.

> He also said, among other things, that when physicians, theologians, and philosophers could not reach a consensus, the judiciary was in no position to speculate.

> On the surface, this seems to be weighty observation, on closer scrutiny, nonsense. I have read that there are more than 3,000 religions in the United States; it would be absurd to expect them to speak with one voice regarding this as they differ on scads of issues.

> What philosophers? One good one might be enough. He didn't name which ones he considered.

> Physicians are bound by medical definitions. If there were no consensus among those turning to medicine it would signify to me that they had poor training. I would expect a good medicine man to explain his opinion based on scientific fact. A medical definition is a scientific fact. Consequently, if all physicians were aware of the definition of embryo, there would not only be consensus, but universal acceptance.

3. Person; a human being as contrasted to an animal or thing. This is found in many dictionaries, but not cited in *Roe v. Wade* or any of the lower cases leading up to *Wade* (See pg 56-57). I claim that the pro-life and government workers who purported to represent the unborn were grossly incompetent for failing to find this in the office dictionary. Perhaps the most popular dictionary at the time of passage of *Roe v. Wade* was *Merriam Webster's Seventh*

New Collegiate Dictionary, which contained that or other similar words. The next edition of *Merriam Webster's* was published in 1973, but omitted the 3-prong definition: repeated attempts to get permission to repeat the definition was rebuffed at the time by a Ms. Goncalves. In the text, I quoted from a *Random House Dictionary* and made reference to the *Seventh* above.

> Recent attempts to secure permission by myself left me stonewalled.

> It seems obvious to me that the editors were fond of *Roe v. Wade* and knew that the definition existed when the case was announced would signal the death of *Wade.* Why else would the publisher of a dictionary deny permission for an author to quote a definition, current at the time a case was handed down?

When abortion law comes before the Supreme Court again, there exist those three sound reasons to believe that the unborn is a constitutional person. This time there will be no escape for the court.

It is forever an embarrassment to the court that all members have seized upon potential life in describing the unborn, resulting in the death of 50 million-plus human beings.

> "Our constitutional watch does not cease mainly because we have spoken before on an issue; when it becomes clear that a prior constitutional interpretation is unsound we are obliged to reexamine the question." (*Planned Parenthood v Casey,* Dissenting opinion of Chief Justice Rehnquist, citations omitted.)

II. Forum

Elsewhere, I have prepared a pattern petition, meaning it would be filed in any and every jurisdiction. I have changed my mind. It should go directly to the Supreme Court in its Original Jurisdiction.

While someone could file an amicus brief, I would recommend another pro-life entity intervene as a party, if that is allowed. If such occurs, I am not encouraging a flood of *amicus* briefs unless the author has something new to say. To simply say that the author agrees with me is stupid as it would be a waste of paper and time.

However, I wouldn't object if there were a large number of persons or entities as interveners in my petition.

III. Planned Parenthood selling body parts

In late July 2015, it was reported that a representative from Planned Parenthood was caught on tape trying to sell body parts of aborted fetuses for profit. Such, if true would be a violation of the law.

Many conservatives were shocked; some liberals were uncomfortable.

One example of an op-ed on the subject can be found in the *Sunday World Herald* July 19, 2015 by Michael Gerson (*The Washington Post*).

ONLINE VIDEO DISPLAYS AN APPALLING TRIVIALIZATION OF LIFE

The full video of the lunch is available online for those willing to risk losing their own. An excerpt:

"I'd say a lot of people want liver," says Nucatola. "And for that reason, most providers will do this case under ultrasound guidance so they'll know where they're putting their forceps. Calvarium – the head – is basically the biggest part. …We've been very good at getting heart, lung, liver, because we know that, so I'm not gonna crush that part. I'm gonna basically crush below. I'm gonna crush above, and I'm gonna see if I can get it all intact. And with the calvarium in general, some people will actually try to change the presentation so that it's not vertex. …So if you do it starting from the breech presentation, there's dialation that happens as the case goes on, and often the last step, you can evacuate an intact, calvarium at the end."

"A lot of people want liver."

Most people think of a zygote as something different from a child. But particularly as technology has allowed us to peer into the womb, human instincts for protection have engaged earlier than nine months. And those who have entirely lost that instinct – including apparently, the Planned Parenthood doctor – seem disconnected from the values of a compassionate society.

In this case, revulsion is not mere sentimentality. It is the sign, and requirement, of our humanity.

The World Herald seems to be a conservative newspaper, but it did print an op-ed by Cecile Richards the president of Planned Parenthood.

VIDEOS' ASSERTIONS ARE FALSE AND EXTREME ATTACK ON WOMEN

By: Cecile Richards

The writer is president of the Planned Parenthood Federation of America. (Special to the Washington Post) Planned Parenthood has been a trusted nonprofit provider of women's health care for nearly a century. Each year, 2.7 million people come to our health centers for high-quality, nonjudgmental, compassionate care.

The most recent attacks in this decades-long campaign represent a new low.

These extremists created a fake business, made apparently misleading corporate filings and then used false government identification to gain access to Planned

Parenthood's medical and research staff with the agenda of secretly filming without consent – then heavily edited the footage to make false and absurd assertions about our standards and services. They spent three years doing everything they could – not to uncover wrongdoing but, rather, to create it. They failed.

While these videos do not show anything illegal on Planned Parenthood's part, medical and scientific conversations can be upsetting to hear, and I immediately apologize for the tone that was used, which did not reflect the compassion that people have come to know and expect from Planned Parenthood.

Some politicians claim that ending support to Planned Parenthood is related to abortion services – knowing full well that because of the Hyde Amendment there has been no federal funding of abortion services except for very narrow exceptions for nearly four decades – and that low-income women have been prevented full access to abortion as a result.

The women who come to Planned Parenthood don't do so to make a political statement; they come to get high-quality, affordable and compassionate care. When a patient comes to us, we don't ask her if she's a Democrat or a Republican because health care provision should never be political.

More than half of Planned Parenthood's health centers are in rural or medically underserved areas. And for many low-income women, Planned Parenthood health centers are their sole source of medical care. Our health centers are lifelines that our country cannot afford to cut.

Whether Congress chooses to stand with extremists or with the women of the United States is up to them. Planned Parenthood will always stand with our patients and protect the rights of every woman to access care. Today, we need the American people to stand with them, too.

If the allegations are indeed true, I can't say that I was appalled as I strongly suspected that Planned Parenthood knew that it was harvesting livers and hearts, etc. These had to be the body parts of human beings. If the Supreme Court through Justice Blackmun's deception was premised on potential life. Planned Parenthood and the local abortion movement, with more skillful lawyers than the pro-life lawyers, were fully aware of the meaning of embryo in the medical dictionary they used the term "products of conception" but no one was shrewd enough to catch them, that these were *human* products of conception. Of course, if the liberal movement revealed this their cause would have been doomed.

I am neither shocked nor appalled if Planned Parenthood did sell as it is ingrained in their long-standing indifference to obvious human life which easily leads to a cavalier approach toward human body parts. Why give the body parts away for expenses when with a little sleight of hand, you could up the ante, who is going to know or care?

The public pulse of the *Omaha World Herald* featured many opinions from its readers on the subject. For years, medical science has relied upon tissues from aborted fetuses and the research has payed dividends and more is expected to come. The following was a front-page feature from the *Omaha World Herald* on August 12, 2015.

UNMC PROUD OF ITS FETAL TISSUE RESEARCH

By Henry J. Cordes

World Herald Staff Writer

The University of Nebraska Medical Center has been among the leading recipients of federal grants for research projects that involve fetal tissue research – exploration that UNMC officials say could soon produce a groundbreaking treatment for Parkinson's disease.

From 2011 through 2014, UNMC received some $5 million in federal funds for research projects that involved some use of fetal tissue, according to an Associated Press database of such research. That ranked UMNMC 14th highest among the 97 research institutions that received such funding during that time.

In addition, the University of Nebraska-Lincoln in 2014 received $500,000 in federal funds for research that also involved fetal tissue, according to an AP database.

The controversy in Washington over Planned Parenthood has again sparked debate over the use of tissue from aborted fetuses for medical research, research that has been used for decades to develop vaccines and medical treatments. The AP reported Tuesday that some $280 million in federally funded research from 2011 to 2014 involved fetal tissue.

UNMC officials say the figures cited in the AP data can be misleading. Only a small portion of the research funded by the competitive federal grants actually uses fetal cells. But UNMC officials said the research has without doubt advanced medicine.

"Research involving fetal cells has led to tremendous advancements in developing treatments for a range of diseases, including Alzheimer's, Parkinson's, AIDS dementia and others," said Tom O' Connor, a UNMC spokesman. "That's why many of the nation's leading research institutions, including the University of Nebraska are responsibly engaged in this type of research."

Much of the work at UNMC has been directed by Dr. Howard Gendelman, who for nearly two decades has led UNMC research into neurodegenerative disorders such as Parkinson's and neuro-infectious diseases like HIV-related dementia.

Gendelman is involved in what UNMC officials called a "groundbreaking human clinical researching trial" that could provide a novel treatment for Parkinson's.

"The idea that led to this research began 16 years ago with fetal cells in a test tube," O' Connor said.

He said UNMC hopes to share the results of the trial later this year.

Other Gendelman research with fetal cells has explored ways to better transport drugs to hard-to-research parts of the body to treat HIV-related dementia. Other UNMC research on HIV involving fetal cells has recently been led by Dr. Jailin Zheng, a professor in pharmacology.

Likewise, the fetal tissue-related research at UNL also is targeting HIV, with chemist Jaintao Guo leading a team seeking an HIV vaccine. Guo's grant had been announced last year, but it had not previously been disclosed to involve fetal tissue.

Controversy erupted in 1999 when it was disclosed that Gendelman had been using fetal tissue in his research, something the university had not previously disclosed. It led for calls from abortion opponents to end the research.

But the NU Board of Regents voted unanimously to support the research, noting the potential to save lives and the chilling effect that a ban would have on research. Efforts in the Legislature to ban the research also subsequently failed. It has continued since.

Since that time, the medical center also has engaged in embryonic stem cell research, another form of controversial research that involves cells taken from embryos.

Reprinted by permission of the Omaha World Herald

Scientists around the nation concur in an article with an associated press byline in the same paper it was stated that if the Universities didn't buy the tissue it would be discarded. It was stated that fetal tissue divide more rapidly than adult cells and adapt to new environments more easily. It would be much slower to identify the causes and come across cures without the unborn tissues.

Many Universities will not name the scientists involved in this research, for their safety in such a highly-charged atmosphere.

Vaccines were created for German Measles, Chicken Pox, Rabies, and Hepatitis A from elective abortions.

If my plan outlined in chapter 2 is followed, stem cell research from fetal tissue will be a thing of the past. My principle approach is likely to result in substantially fewer than the million plus abortions that occur in the United States each year.

If abortions are drastically reduced in this country, I would expect a broad ripple effect in many parts of the world.

IV. The Book of Job

First things first, although no one seems to know it but me, the old testament allows for liberal abortion—for the spiritual and physical benefit of the unborn; but practically speaking that isn't feasible. My source is Job, the man, often applauded but not necessarily understood in several significant respects.

In my view, Job stands out over all other figures as the most outstanding person in the *Old Testament*. He was sinless his whole life. A rich man with a large number of children, he believed or feared that they spent too much time partying.

As stated Job was an innocent man. Satan, in wandering around the world noticed Job, a servant of God. Satan challenged God to take away the shield around Job who would then turn against and reject God.

God placed Job at Satan's mercy. He was allowed to do anything rotten short of taking Job's life.

Within a short period of time, Job lost all of his belongings and then his children. His wife urged him to curse God. Job's response was "The Lord giveth, and the Lord taketh away."

Job developed severe marks or pocks and suffered severely for a long time, but the bible does not state how long. The bulk of the book is an alternating dialogue with three friends. The nub of the matter was that each of the three endeavored to convince Job that he suffered because he sinned. The individuals went back and forth, they could not convince Job he was a sinner; he could not convince them that he was a totally innocent man.

In the discourses, Job kept asking for, even demanding, an audience with God to show he was innocent.

At length God did show up "In a whirlwind" asking why Job was making such a noise. He pointed out to Job that he was not around during the creation so there was much he didn't know. Ultimately God indicated that this was not it, the time or place, to answer Job's concerns.

He did praise Job for saying the truth about Him, and asked Job to forgive the three that were not truthful. God blessed and rewarded Job with a very long life, and three daughters.

From my perspective all of Job is profound, consider all of Chapter 3:

After this opened Job his mouth, and cursed his day.

2 And Job spake, and said,

3 Let the day perish wherein I was born, and the night in *which* it was said, There is a man child conceived.

4 Let that day be darkness; let not God regard it from above, neither let the light shine upon it.

5 Let darkness and the shadow of death stain it; let a cloud dwell upon it; let the blackness of the day terrify it.

6 As for that night, let darkness seize upon it; let it not be joined unto the days of the year, let it not come into the number of the months.

7 Lo, let that night be solitary, let no joyful voice come therein.

8 Let them curse it that curse the day, who are ready to raise up their mourning.

9 Let the stars of the twilight thereof be dark; let it look for light, but have none; neither let it see the dawning of day:

10 Because it shut not up the doors of my mother's womb, nor hid sorrow from mine eyes.

11 Why died I not from the womb? Why did I not give up the ghost when I came out of the belly?

12 Why did the knees prevent me? Or why the breasts that I should suck?

13 For now should I have lain still and been quiet, I should have slept: then and I been at rest,

14 With kings and counsellors of the earth, which built desolate places for themselves;

15 Or with princes that had gold, who filled their houses with silver;

16 Or as an hidden untimely birth I had not been; as infants which never saw light.

17 There the wicked cease from troubling; and there the weary be at rest.

18 There the prisoners rest together; they hear not the voice of the oppressor.

19 The small and great are there; and the servant is free from his master.

20 Wherefore is light given to him that is in misery, and life unto the bitter in soul;

21 Which long for death, but it cometh not; and dig for it more than for hid treasures;

22 Which rejoice exceedingly, and are glad, when they can find the grave?

23 Why is light given to a man whose way is hid, and whom God hath hedged in?

24 For my sighing cometh before I eat, and my roarings are poured out like the waters.

25 For the thing which I greatly feared is come upon me, and that which I was afraid of is come unto me.

26 I was not in safety, neither had I rest, neither was I quiet; yet trouble came.

From his perspective, it would have been better not to have been born. Since God praised him for telling the truth, being still-born is perhaps better than living a life full of misery. Compare Verse 16 in *The*

New Jerusalem Bible; "or, put away like an abortive child, I should not have existed, like little ones that never see that light."

Arguably, both versions could refer to miscarriages, but then again, an abortion would prevent suffering, just as would a still-birth

Consider Matthew 7:24-27:

> "Therefore, everyone who listens to these words of mine and acts on them will be like a sensible man who built his house on a rock. Rain came down, floods rose, gales blew and hurled themselves against that house, and it did not fall: it was founded on rock. But everyone who listens to these words of mine and does not act on them will be like a stupid man who built his house on sand. Rain came down, floods rose, gales blew and struck that house, and it fell; and what a fall it had."

It is my interpretation that all 50 million aborted children have a free ticket to heaven. Consequently, it is my positon that God is not opposed to abortion for any reason, but that it is contrary to a correct analysis of the United States Constitution.

However, I believe it's impossible to inject religion to end abortion controversy. I think that a pregnant woman would have a conflict of interest were she to claim her right to abort on behalf of the child's soul. Similarly, no one else would have standing (especially a Pastor). cf. THE THIRD TESTAMENT part one The God of Daniel religion (2016) pg. 57.

In any event it would be preposterous to think that any American tribunal would rule any abortion acceptable if it would lead to the child's automatic entry into heaven.

V. The United States Supreme Court

On June 27, 2016 the Supreme Court ruled that two restrictions in a Texas abortion statute placed an undue burden on a woman's right to have an abortion.

One was called the *"admitting privileges requirement,"* whereby a physician performing an abortion is to have acting admitting privileges at a hospital located no more than 30 miles away. The second was called *"the surgical-center requirement,"* whereby the abortion facility had to meet the minimum standards for the ambulatory surgical centers.

Both sections were struck down on a five to three vote (*Whole Women's Health v. Hellar Stadt, 579 US 2016*). As all members remain in the dark about Blackmun's lie, nothing would be served by discussing the case in detail.

VI. Prayer

Based upon what I said in division IV, it inevitably follows that the pro-life organizations don't speak for God. If they were aware of chapter 3 of Job, they might not be so fanatical.

I've got a bone to pick with them, what I consider a very large bone. They like to hold street demonstrations and public rallies, especially on the anniversary of *Roe v Wade*. They also have their "celebrate life" banquets. A common feature of these activities is prayer, public prayer.

Jesus said:

> "And when you pray, do not imitate the hypocrites: they like to say their prayers standing up in the synagogues and at street corners for people to see them. In truth I tell you they have had their reward, but when you pray, go to your private room, shut yourself in, and so pray to your Father who is in that secret place, and your Father who sees all that is done in secret will reward you." (Matthew 6: 5-6)

Jesus goes on to say: "do not babble," by using many words, simply say the Lord's Prayer: "Your Father knows what you need before you ask him." (Verse 9-10)

In November 26, 2016 I self-published *THE THIRD TESTAMENT: part 1,* mentioned above, in which I indicate that God is appalled at what takes place in all of the churches.

CHAPTER 2: My proposal for the future of Abortion Laws, Policy, and Practices

Once it is realized that *Roe v. Wade* is totally devoid of principle because of premise on a lie, the crucial point of the decision, the case can safely be ignored. This lie has fostered more than 50 million abortions since January 1973 then comprised of crimes of the 20th and 21st century. It necessarily follows that the companion case *Doe v. Bolton* giving physicians and hospitals the right to perform abortions *carte blanche* also falls.

In the lead opinion, Justice Blackmun stated that if the constitutional personhood of the unborn were established, the claim of a pregnant woman seeking an abortion "collapses." I think that this is an overstatement as could be shown there can be situations where an abortion can be approved. The defeat of *Wade* and *Doe v. Bolton* seems preordained once the court receives official notice of the judicial corruption.

In the meantime, I suggest that the State Medical Associations and Societies take the matter into their own hands by preparing a uniform code of ethics, one that will be duplicated in each American jurisdiction, a policy and practice to implemented under the code. This can be done independently of State Legislature which I am also recommending. The medical profession is risking wholesale litigation unless it immediately abandons the "ethics" that the now discredited *Bolton* provided for.

Leading the charge, I hope, will be the combined forces of the entire pro-life communities. They've long waited to oust *Wade* and *Bolton*; now I give them the opportunity based on principle.

I. Code of Ethics

The first order of business is to establish a code of ethics which considers all possibilities, based on principle.

Principle #1

When certain fundamental rights are involved, interference with these rights may be justified only upon a compelling interest. *Roe v. Wade, 410 U.S. 113, 115* (1973). While the decision is filled with gobbledygook and garbage, this gem though hidden, sparkles.

Principle #2

Life is the most fundamental of fundamental rights and should be considered the first right of any human being (McTaggart, *Abortion and the Outlaw* (2000 Notes Added) 145). There exists a strong presumption that an unborn child at any stage of pregnancy has this right to life. There also exists a competing interest in the woman and preserving her life if in jeopardy.

Principle #3

Most women who are pregnant are happy about it so they eagerly anticipate birth. Some women may want an abortion. The following shall be considered.

a. For reasons personal to her, she believes she will have a better chance of pursuing happiness than if she doesn't have the abortion; this never overrides the unborn's right to be born alive.
b. Pregnancy and birth may be dangerous to her health. However defined, this is never a legitimate basis for abortion.
c. Continued pregnancy and birth may be likely to destroy her life. Again, I think this calls for the opinion of a competent physician, none of whom is the abortionist.
d. Two physicians may believe that the child will be born severely mentally or physically defective. An issue is whether such condition is likely to substantially interfere with the child's right to pursue happiness if born alive. If so, this may be an indication that an abortion is warranted. Recent reports from Florida indicate an outbreak of Zika whereby the pregnant woman is bitten by a mosquito, resulting in a child deformed, usually brain damaged. The pursuit of happiness principle governs.
e. The pregnant woman has no right to "liberty" as held in *Planned Parenthood v. Casey* as an abortion always interferes with the life of another human being.

   f. The woman has no right of "privacy" as this tantamount to killing a child in a clinic or hospital. Justice Rehnquist pointed this out in his dissent in *Roe v. Wade.*

   g. An abortion may not be approved because it's believed to be beneficial to the unborn's soul.

Principle #4

The unborn has the right to be heard in every case in which an abortion is requested by a pregnant woman or her physician. In each instance the child shall have a guardian-ad-litem, someone who is thought to advance the best interests of the child. This individual shall be medically trained, thereby eliminating most attorneys.

Principle #5

If the pregnant woman declares that she wants an abortion because of rape or incest, this should never be allowed, even though pregnancy might be very aggravating. In most cases placement for adoption is an acceptable option.

Principle #6

There may be an unknown consideration, the *Bible.* While the book of Job may sanction an abortion for preservation of a child's soul, no guardian-at-litem would ever be able to speak on behalf of the child's soul, nor would any court ever be in a position to adjudicate as a measure of saving a child's soul.

Principle #7

In considering life versus life, the woman's past history may be evaluated as a guide as to her likelihood to pursuing happiness.

Principle #8

The father, if known, must have the opportunity to be heard, if interested, in any and every case with respect to her request for an abortion. However, if the pregnancy resulted from rape or incest the putative father's opinion shall ordinarily be given little weight.

Principle #9

Every physician who wishes to express an opinion has the right to be heard. The physician intending to perform the procedure shall not be the woman's sole advocate.

Principle #10

The State's Medical Association Ethics Committee, shall make guidelines as to how late in pregnancy an abortion may be had. It is my opinion that this decision rest with the person deciding whether an abortion shall be approved in a given case. I've never read any of the cases on partial-birth abortion. While I don't believe in late-term abortion, I yield to physicians to make the call. In other words, I am not comfortable in making a decision as I am not well-informed.

It seems as though the last few years, conservative legislatures have placed the line of demarcation at 20 weeks, the point at which an unborn is believed to suffer pain if aborted.

The Committee might determine to postpone a decision on the guideline, deferring to the appointed hearing officer to make a decision.

Principle #11

I would state that the methods of approved abortions be established as follows:

a. An abortion may be performed only in a hospital authorized by state law or medical clinic approved by the hearing officer.
b. An abortion by use of the RU486 pill shall not be permitted.
c. The morning after pill shall (or if the committee so decides) shall not be permitted.

II. Medical Ethicist

The ethics committee of the State Medical Association or Society must first establish a Medical Ethicist who shall determine whether under which circumstances an abortion may be permitted. The committee shall consider Part I, stated above, and shall adopt it or create a code that it determines more suitable.

The ethics committee shall appoint an ethics chairperson or medical ethicist.

1. The person appointed shall be a person respected as being ethical (willing to abide by the code of ethics and having a reputation of being fair-minded).

2. A second qualification is having a knowledge and understanding of principles of equity that are part of every legal system in the United States, I think. If the person selected has no experience in equity issues presented in court historically, he or she would be required to study the basic questions and seek legal advice and counsel from an attorney so experienced.

3. The individual may be a physician, but not necessarily, a judge (retired); it is thought that active judges are often overworked in many jurisdictions and may not have the time for reflection on all aspects of the case.

4. The person so appointed shall have the position for 1 year. A copy of every decision he or she makes shall be forwarded to the Medical Ethics Committee. Any party or physician objecting to any decision may file a grievance with the committee. If the committee deems the complaints, upon investigation, reveal that replacement prior to the year's end would be in the best interests of society, may interview the hearing officer and replace him or her for as little as an appearance of impropriety or inability to properly observe the code of ethics and equity principles.

5. The person appointed shall have had no prior interest as either a pro-life or pro-choice advocate even though the party may have beliefs that one side or the other had the better position.

6. If after 11 months have expired and the committee is satisfied with the performance of the person, in that state the person may hold that position indefinitely.

7. The title of the hearing officer, designated by the Committee shall be medical ethicist.

8. As it is anticipated that there will be few abortions sought there shall be just one medical ethicist for each state, unless the committee deems it necessary to establish more than one.

9. The guardian-ad-litem is one whose sole interest is the best interest of the child. He or she need not be a physician, and I would suggest that very few attorneys are qualified by training or experience. The individual may have been a pro-life advocate in the past and shall be appointed by the hearing officer. If the hearing officer determines that the guardian-at-litem is overzealous to the point of not respecting the Code of Ethics, the medical ethicist shall have the sole power to remove or replace.

10. A request for an abortion will ordinarily be initiated by the pregnant woman or her physician. She shall tell her physician. She shall tell her physician the reason she is seeking an abortion. By separate report the physician shall express his or her own opinion based upon the understanding of the code of ethics. Then the guardian-ad-litem shall be given a copy of the request, which will go out to the father, if known, and all physicians expected to be interested, including whether facilities are and a qualified abortionist is available in the vicinity.

III. Policy

1. The process began when a physician notifies the medical ethicist in writing, providing in detail why it is believed that continued pregnancy will endanger the pregnant woman's life. No other grounds are a justification, unless it is believed that the child I born would be so defective that it would not be able to pursue happiness The medical ethicist shall forthwith a second physician who shall report back in detail. The medical ethicist has the discretion to appoint a third physician.

2. If going forward, the medical ethicist shall appoint a guardian-ad-litem for the unborn child.

3. The father, may align himself with the mother's physician or the child's guardian-ad litem.

4. The hearing shall be conducted entirely on written reports which could be distributed by fax or e-mail.
5. Expenses related to the hearing shall be borne by the State Medical Society or Association.
6. Within a reasonable time, not to exceed seven business days, the medical ethicist shall file a written order containing finding of facts, analysis of governing principles and conclusion. The names of the individuals shall not be disclosed.
7. The order of the medical ethicist shall be a public record and disseminated to all state medical organizations (Hopefully the American Medical Association will assist with distribution).
8. If on abortion is authorized by the medical ethicist, the costs shall be the responsibility of the woman and the father (to be decided by the medical ethicist).
9. The medical ethicist shall have full authority to oversee that the abortion occur as soon as possible, if that is the order.
10. No party has the right to appeal.

IV. Procedure

1. The hearing shall be conducted entirely on written reports, which could easily be faxed and/or e-mailed.
2. The hearing shall be heard within 20 days.
    a. By a day certain each individual wishing to be heard must file a written report, with a copy (forwarded to all interested) parties.
    b. Seven days later, all will have an opportunity to respond.
    c. If the hearing officer has questions of one or more parties, he should forward a copy to all, enabling the others to respond if so desired.
    d. The hearing officer shall issue his order as soon as possible.

No party has the right to appeal.

As the guardian-ad-litem, the physicians, and the hearing officer are all professionals, no reason exists to have a Super Review Board, which probably wouldn't be any more qualified or competent.

Courts have demonstrated that judges and lawyers have botched considerations of abortion since the beginning. They have neither training nor experience. They waste an awful lot of time and still come down with decisions not based on principle. Thus, the first state to adopt a code of ethics and principles to appoint and guide a medical ethicist shall be forwarded to American Medical Association which shall forthwith send the same to all state medical associations and societies.

V. Uniformity

I would argue that if one state devises a good code of ethics, all other states should follow suit. While I don't make them, my suggested approach is an unusual but appropriate forum under the circumstances.

If the first one to do so comes up with a better approach than I propose, that is acceptable to me. As *Roe v. Wade* and *Doe v. Bolton* are bad law, a state medical authority should immediately implement the proposals set forth above even in the absence of state legislation.

VI. State Legislation

I recommend uniformity in all state laws. I suggest:

Any abortion in this state is a felony, punishable by life imprisonment unless approved by the State Medical Society or Association.

Just as judges and lawyers are incompetent to make just and wise decisions on matters of abortion, state lawmakers-as demonstrated by the wide divergence of laws-are incompetent to make principled decisions. Because of compromise and bowing to outside pressure, they come up with differing laws.

The right to abortion should not be based on a collection of legislatures, rather should, as much as possible, be the same throughout the country.

VII. Unauthorized Abortions

An abortion not authorized by this ethics code shall be punished according to law. The consenting pregnant woman and whoever aids an illegal abortion shall be prosecuted as aiders and abettors as defined by state law.

While it is believed that the unsafe, illegal practice of abortions may result in some maternal injuries or deaths, the number is likely to be far less than the number of persons killed as authorized by *Roe v. Wade* and *Planned Parenthood v. Casey.*

As stated at the beginning, the right to life is the most fundamental of the fundamental rights. Birth and adoption are reasonable outcomes of pregnancies lasting 9 months. It may seem cruel to require pregnancies by rape to be carried to term, a number of people suffer from their own control of circumstances; e.g. cancer, epilepsy, and diabetes.

VIII. The Number of Abortions Radically Diminish

The Department of Health and Human Services has reported that less than one percent of abortions are performed to preserve the life of the pregnant woman. This means that, at the very least, not more than 10,000 abortions per year. Due to the Department's lack of disclosing the actual figures the amount may be substantially less than this figure. Presently, most abortions performed in the United States are for maternal health. Accordingly, considering there are 50 States affected, the numbers are to be greatly diminished, perhaps less than 1,000 or even less than 100. If there is a change in the United States policy and practice it may have a ripple effect worldwide.

IX. The Promised Land in Sight.

If my proposal is implemented, I expect there will be one hearing officer for the entire state and there will be very few abortions, as stated earlier.

Abortion clinics will not be able to afford to stay in business; I don't know about the competency of physicians who have not done, and don't want to do, abortions. Some may disagree with ethics code implemented on the belief that it is contrary to their religion; the same for hospitals.

a. My paper hearing provides for due process, in my opinion, for all-the rights to be heard under unique circumstances. There is little time for appeal, and little to be gained.
b. My paper hearing provides for equal protection. All parties similarly situated in all states operate under the same rules. What goes in Nebraska goes in Iowa and California, and so on.
c. The pursuit of happiness may be asserted by all these parties:
    1. Pregnant woman
    2. Unborn child as represented by guardian-ad-litem
    3. Father, if known
d. A new principle seems to be announced in the recent DOMA case concerning "gays dignity." Mother, father, and child are deserving of being respected.

But, as the child is unwanted, someone will have to lose in this competition. I stated early on, life is the most fundamental of rights, so that the burden on the mother wishing to rebut this presumption may rarely or never be met.

Whatever happens, do not over complicate Blackmun committed one simple lie. Its exposure is sufficient to erase the most monumental blunder in jurisdiction history.

CHAPTER 3 Intentional Abuse of Words by Justices Blackmun and Roberts

In my view, the best and greatest writer of the English language in history was John Locke, a physician by training and practice. I say best and greatest because his work sparked action and reaction in several areas. In religion, for example, he wrote four letters on intoleration. These had an immediate impact, the cessation of religious wars in Europe (he wrote around the year 1700). Also, *Treatise on Government, First Essay, Treatise on Government, Second Essay.* The latter was said to have been the most significant influence leading to the American Revolution. In *UCKING POWER (sic)* (2008), the subtitle was John Locke and the United States

Constitution. He expressed some principles of law still undiscovered but which if injected would lead to modifications in society. Oddly enough, I could not find a single American judicial case quoting or citing him. I found extensive support, both in that work and in his *Concerning Human Understanding* has never been improved upon in my estimation. These writings are considered classics, contained in volume 35 of the Greatest Books in the Western World series.

Abortion and the Outlaw 1987, Notes added 1989, Notes added 2000, 2001 and the chapters in this book lead to one conclusion: his continual gross abuse of words was intentional. Justice White called it "raw judicial power."

While Justice Blackmun B.S.'ed about all kinds of opinions and the impossibility of finding consensus, "at this point in time," by the judiciary, he made the following statement:

> The pregnant woman cannot be isolated in her privacy. She carries an embryo and later a fetus, if one accepts the medical definition of the developing young in the human uterus. See *Dorland's Illustrated Medical Dictionary* 478-479, 547 (20th Ed. 1965) (quoted at *Abortion and the Outlaw*, 144) *Roe v. Wade*, 410 U.S. 113, 162 (1973).

To Justice Blackmun: Of course one must accept the "definition of the developing young in the human uterus." Courts have no right to reject definitions as recognized sources. Rambling on about positions and views of certain groups, he had before his very eyes, the definition that the embryo was a human organism from one week after conception. A human organism is a human being. My only conclusion is that Blackmun shrewdly omitted the key word in the definition (Neither Justice White nor the other justices caught this "Abuse of Words"). I will now quote that word that Blackmun had to have seen, which I didn't discover until March 1, 2000.

> The early or developing stage of any organism, especially the developing product of fertilization of an egg. In the human, the embryo is generally considered to be the developing organism from one week after conception to the end of the second month. *Dorland's Dictionary 547.*

Without arguing it, I've concluded that Blackmun was very dishonest. There is not a hint of "potential" to this definition. He deceived the court, the country, and the world. Paraphrasing to the detriment of the unborn is unconceivable. That alone should prompt A RE-EXAMINATION OF *Wade*. While he knew it was an emotional case, he failed to provide a single definition. To this day, most of the justices refer to the unborn as a potential human being. And there were definitions available to the unborn from the standard dictionary:

a. A recently born or unborn child (Blackmun recognized that you can call the unborn a child but neglected, apparently, to realize that that made the unborn a person.) See 410 U.S. at 153.

b. If you look up child in the dictionary, you can find the definition for child-bearing: of or relating to the process of conceiving, being pregnant with and giving birth to children. With the process of conceiving-at this time-it is a child.

c. Embryo: The developing human individual from the time of implantation to the end of the eighth week after conception.

d. Person: A human being as opposed to animal or thing. This is not contained in all dictionaries. Some have it or a slight variation, include: from *Random House Dictionary* (1967); *Webster`s Third New World Dictionary* (1996); see also *7th Oxford Dictionary* and *Webster's 7th New Collegiate Dictionary*, and is included in all those huge volumes found in libraries. See also the current edition for *Dorland's Illustrated Medical Dictionary* (28th ed. 1994) 542 which will be quoted of shortly. Originally, Aristotle declared the unborn started as a plant, then animal, then human. His classifications are still valid today, but not the specific applications to the unborn to state otherwise we would have to ask: is it a plant? Is it an animal? This 3-world definition can be taken from *Dorland's* current definition of, Embryo: 1. In plants...2. In animals...3. In humans, developing organism from the end of the second week after fertilization to the end of the eighth week.

In the definitions considered here, we don't have to look at the remaining list of errors that I totaled at 30. This is the crux of the case.

As far as I can tell, this is the only time in history that a United States Supreme Court Justice has abused his power by rambling on about numerous irrelevant viewpoints and positions, and carefully mentioning definitions and failing to state the only one that was plainly in his sight as it was in his cite, "a human organism."

In referring to the definition and not providing it, he deceived Justice White and the others. I'm 100% sure that if Justice White or his law clerks looked up the definition in *Dorland's* themselves, they would have blasted him for his sly dishonesty.

As suggested above, I have no other case where a Supreme Court Justice has butchered a definition.

The Harvard-trained Justice Roberts, in *Sebelius*, in construing penalty as a tax, abused his power, but this seemed to be pure stupidity, not knowing the essential principles of judging as expounded by Cardozo.

In any event, I believe I'm the first one in history to charge and prove dishonesty and corruption by a Supreme Court justice. While he is not alive to defend himself, his intentional sliding over the medical definition which he looked at and cited cannot be defended.

By and large, it was the true "crime of the 20th century" as it triggered the death of millions upon millions of human beings without due process of law. And now it continues on to be the "crime of the 21st century."

The only ones who cared were the many pro-lifers. Their attorneys will forever be branded incompetent, and rightly so for failing to examine the numerous shortcomings of *Wade* in great detail.

Most physicians did not respond to my two post-*Wade* surveys.

Thus, the point I was trying to make was confirmed: most physicians do not claim to be experts on abortion and many more are indifferent.

At this time, I turn to the estimable John Locke. His *Treatise on Government, Second Essay* paved the way to the American Revolution. His *Letters Concerning Toleration* resulted in a cessation of religious warfare in the 17th Century. Here I am concerned with a portion of the classic, *Concerning Human Understanding* and how some of us misuse language. After I have listed the most common six abuses, I will briefly apply them to Justices Blackmun and Roberts.

CONCERNING HUMAN UNDERSTANDING

BOOK III – OF WORDS

Of the Abuse of Words

"(T)here are several *willful* faults and neglect where men are guilty of in this way of communication."

I. *"Some words introduced without clear ideas annexed to them, even in their first original."* These, for the most part, the several sects of philosophy and religion have introduced." For example, **transubstantiation.**

II. *"Other words, to which ideas were annexed at first, used afterwards without distinct meanings."* "Men take the words they find in use among their neighbors; and that they may not seem ignorant what they stand for, use them confidently, without troubling their heads about a certain fixed meaning, whereby besides the ease of it, they obtain this advantage, that, as in such discourses they seldom are in the right, so they are as seldom to be convinced that they are in the wrong; it being all one to go about to draw these men out of their mistakes who have not settled notions, as to dispossess, a vagrant of his habitation who has no settled abode.

III. *"Affected obscurity, is in the Peripatetic and other sects of philosophy. Thirdly,* another abuse of language is an *affected obscurity*; by either applying old words to new and unusual significations; or using new and unusual significations; or introducing new and ambiguous terms, without defining either; or else putting them together, as many confound their ordinary meaning."

IV. *"By taking words for things. Fourthly,* another great abuse of words, is the taking them for things."

V. *"By setting them in the place of what they cannot signify. Fifthly, another abuse of words is setting them in the place of things which they do or can by no means signify."*

VI. *"By proceeding upon the supposition that the words we use have a certain and evident signification which other men cannot but understand. Sixthly,* there remains another more general, though perhaps less observed, abuse of words; and that is, that men by having by a long and familiar use annexed to them certain ideas, they are apt to imagine *so near and necessary connection between the names and signification they use them in*, that they forwardly suppose one cannot but understand what their meaning is . . ."

Justice Blackmun wrote that the unborn was not a "person in the whole sense." 410 U.S. at 162. This phrase had never been used before, was a creation of his imagination. In legal terms, or otherwise, there is no person in the whole sense. This would clearly be a violation of definitions I, III, V and VI. See *Abortion and the Outlaw*, Daniel McTaggart (Emerson, NE: DeLago Press 1989) 67-69.

Potential life. Justice Blackmun could not reach the conclusion that the unborn was a person or human being. This was a violation of Locke's definitions I and II.

"Embryo and fetus." While referring to both definitions and not distinguishing them was a violation of definition II by Blackmun.

Chief Justice Robert's substitution of tax for penalty violated definitions II, III, V, and VI.

As suggested earlier, the great Justice Cardozo must be turning in his grave by this unprecedented turn of judicial events.

CHAPTER 4: Abuse of Words by Dictionaries

When I wrote *Abortion and the Outlaw*, I used the *Webster's Seventh New Colligate Dictionary*. I wanted to quote the following definition of person: "A human being as distinguished from an animal or thing." I think it was definition 2B.

I wrote for permission from *Merriam-Webster* to quote it. I had several letters back and forth from Ms. Goncalves, Permissions Edition. She wouldn't give me permission. She said she would only give permission to quote from the next edition which had deleted the pertinent definition (I am sure I didn't make copies of my correspondence, but I suppose I might be able to find her letters if I looked).

But it is unnecessary.

On August 24, 2012, I wrote the following letter in handwriting (and kept a copy).

Permissions Editor
Merriam-Webster's Collegiate Dictionary
Merriam-Webster, Inc.
Springfield, MA

Dear Permissions Editor:

In 1986 and 1987 you refused permission to quote "person" 2B in the 7th Edition in *Abortion and the Outlaw*. Unfortunately, I no longer have the correspondence, the volume or the precise definition.

now requesting permission to use the definition along with an editorial comment from you as to why the definition was deleted. I would use the definition in a court case. Please provide me with the definition.

The court case concerns *Roe v. Wade* and that definition was current when *Wade* was decided. So it is a historically correct definition.

Sincerely,
Dan McTaggart

In a letter dated August 29, 2012, I received a response from Stephen J. Perrault, Director of Defining. He pointed out that in that there was no "2a and 2b" *Webster's Seventh New Collegiate Dictionary* © 1963 in his handwriting and page 848 *Webster's New Collegiate Dictionary* © 1973.

I discovered that what I was looking for was (1b, end quote that it was not contained in the 1973 edition.

At the time, I was very puzzled about why Ms. Goncalves's permission was limited to the next edition, which curiously shows that the *Seventh New Collegiate Dictionary* was succeeded by *Webster's New Collegiate Dictionary*. As dictionaries are about words, it should have logically followed that the next edition would be the eighth edition.

While I can't be considered an expert on dictionaries, I have always thought that definitions are either added on or declared obsolete, but not deleted.

As I have been stonewalled by *Merriam-Webster*, no response to my September 4, 2012 letter. I presume that the editors were corrupt for deleting such an obvious definition that other dictionaries have— especially when I alerted them that it was crucial.

September 4, 2012

Steven J. Perrault
Director of Defining
Merriam-Webster, Inc.
Springfield, MA 01102

Dear Sir:

Thank you for your response to me on August 29, 2012.

You are correct. My recollection was faulty.

I am requesting permission to quote definition 1b and 1c from the *Webster's Seventh New Collegiate Dictionary*.

Sincerely,
Dan McTaggart

I have yet to receive a response from this letter

When I looked for other sources, I looked for dictionaries that were current as of 1973 and I found *Random House* (1967). I think I miss-cited the *Oxford Dictionary* which had a similar definition (I'm not sure).

It seems as though *Merriam-Webster* publishes a new addition every few years, which I find to be both stupid and a rip-off to the consumers. If there are new definitions over a period of time, they should logically be placed in a pocket part so the reader will readily be able to consider what is new.

I may be the first person in history to presume that an editor or group of editors of a standard and popular dictionary are corrupt.

CHAPTER 5: On Abortion and the Outlaw:
A Trashy Book about a Trashy Subject:
A Pot at the End of the Rainbow

When I wrote Abortion and the Outlaw in 1987, I ran out of funding and could no longer pay for final publication.

In July 1989 while in Norfolk Regional Center, I received Social Security benefits. My mother, Catherine McTaggart, was named payee.

Although, I think some family members were opposed, she permitted me to publish. I think I tried to contact the South Sioux City (or Dakota Country) Star which advertised that it will provide such service. The ultimate quack, James O'Sullivan, psychiatrist, assumed that I was writing to complain about life at NRC and wouldn't let the letter be sent. From this point on, I wasn't allowed to send any letters unless they were first screened by a nurse. The practice was put in effect and lasted until I was discharged.

I contacted a printer on Hamilton Street in Sioux City. The entity agreed to publish 2,000 books for $2,600. It had been preprinted by a business in Lincoln, Nebraska, for which I paid $3,000, I believe. The manager of that business told me that the firm could do the ultimate printing for either $3,000 or $3,900, I forget which.

A binder in Lincoln quoted me $2 a copy for a hard cover.

Thus, I thought the $2,600 quote was acceptable (As I've found out since, there exist many firms who will let self-publish, perhaps cheaper, definitely better).

The Hamilton Street printer contacted me and said that although we hadn't discussed cover, she would include one at no additional cost.

One of the staff members at NRC was an artist of sorts and I reached an agreement for him to design the cover. Three roses were sketched on the upper right hand corner as I was pretty sure that roses were associated with the anti-abortion forces.

On the middle, center-left was a wolf and a tree which I would call a Christmas tree. The wolf was my symbol for the hunted outlaw-unborn title. The printer also sketched.

Abortion
and the
Outlaw

On the cover.

I gave copies to friends, signed, numbered, and dated. I kept a list of names, but no addresses. While I thought it a good and important book, I figured it would be boring to read for anyone who was not interested in abortion and found very few friends who were.

I sent the first two copies to Justice Blackmun and Justice White, who I thought wrote the best opinion in *Roe v. Wade*.

I sent copies to various state and national leaders in the pro-life community. They all shunned me. I was shocked.

I think I sold 20 to 25 copies over the years. One pro-life editor reviewed it in his monthly magazine. He called me and told me that the book fell apart (My agreement with the Hamilton Street printer said nothing about binding). They agreed to punch holes, with the top and middle holes of a 3-ring binder. It was my plan to put it (5 ½ x 8") in a 8 ½ x 11" binder.

I decided that was too trashy and too bulky and too costly.

I bought some string, but that proved to be very stupid and totally unworkable.

In punching holes, the printer was sometimes careless and didn't make a perfect fit for the three ring binders. So, I had her repunch, which meant that the center had a ½ punch hole. Thus, when I turned to the fasteners, they weren't big enough. The result was to put two fasteners, one from each side. This process resulted in a firmly bound book. So, if you get one, be glad.

The books were delivered in 17 boxes. At first, I had them stocked in the small bedroom of the mobile home I was living in. I moved them to Patsy Henderson, now Knecht's house. When she sold her house and moved, I transported all of them to the Bill and Janelle McTaggart farm southwest of Emerson. While I was in The Norfolk Regional Center (Continually and Illegally), a water pipe broke. When I returned there, I remember that I discovered that most were soaked. It was a major harassment carrying all those heavy water soaked packed boxes out to an incinerator or wired circle for burning. They were too wet to burn them then. Not all of them were soaked, so I ended up renting a part of a former car wash east of Mike's Grocery Store in Emerson. Mike McFarland owned both.

Over time, most of the books were destroyed by dust. In disgust, I got Mike's permission to throw the rest in his dumpster.

So now I have approximately 50 books left.

I have the original copies in 6 X 9" manila envelopes. I am not going to open them and lift out the books. Some end on page 130, as originally published in 1989. I don't know, but it is possible that some have Year 2000 and 2001 notes up to page 147.

It is my intention to have printed exactly enough pages to make it a complete book. These pages contain more than any conventional publisher would allow. They were prepared by a temporary husband and wife business in South Sioux City, Nebraska. I wasn't given the opportunity to read the pages before they were printed. I think I was their only customer. I'm pretty sure that with my work, they went out of business. I'm also pretty sure that he told me "no charge." I was on a very restricted budget. I didn't argue with him.

In any event, if a seller distributes only the first 130 pages, he/she must take down the names and address of the purchasers to mark or otherwise deliver the remaining pages when they are available.

Current Possessors of Abortion and the Outlaw

A. Purchasers

The author believes that 20 to 25 copies have been sold over the years, but knows the identity of very few. As there were no conditions placed on the purchasers, it would be unfair to impose restrictions at this point.

B. Gift Recipients

In the early years, I recorded the names (but no addresses) of those that received this book as a gift. I have long ago lost this list.

I didn't give out the book to persuade friends and relatives. Not a single recipient has given me a critique, except I think Steve Runty and Paul McCallum did in a letter to me undated, but I think it was 2002, after the year 2000 and 2001 notes were printed and distributed.

I think that I had 200 copies printed but my mind is a blank as to the extent to which I distributed them.

I'm sure that the time I was, as now, living in poverty. It seems to me that the cost of mailing was $0.50. apiece.

As copyright holder, I authorize you to photo and sell. But I expect that advertising expenses may make it cost-ineffective. The pro-life networks are undoubtedly well-organized, so that would be an outlet or network.

If you are not interested in the subject of abortion, selling it would be a sensible way of getting cash. If you do sell, I would like you to inform me that name, number and date and color of handwriting.

It seems to me that the first 40 or so were done with a green magic marker (But I may be mistaken on this point). If you do sell and report to me, I may_no will_report to others what you got, as that may give inquirers a gauge for estimating the value of the book.

The name I used isn't important at all. The number is what I, as a purchaser, would value the most. It seems like the #1 is Bernal Herrera Chavarria, San Jose, Costa Rica. Altogether, I believe I sent 12 copies to him with no instructions as to how or whom to distribute to. It seems to me he told me he gave one to a cousin that I met who was a college professor. The pay offered to take me on a jungle safari in Costa Rica (I didn't tell him that I was afraid I'd encounter spiders).

Anyway, I'm pretty sure that Bernal later told me the professor died. I don't remember asking the cause, I don't think he was very old.

Most of my close relatives were next in line. I remember signing copies for Patsy Henderson, now Knecht, the day of her husband Mort's funeral- for all of the kids. (I think there are 8.) By that time (I have no idea of what year) but as to numbers, I kind of winged it and used the 160 range, I believe.

In any event, I'm asking that you, donees if you do sell to give me a 10% "non-repayable loan" written on the check. That is consistent with the Bible, is not income to me, and is not tax deductible. Luke 6:34

I'm requesting George Kubat give me an opinion as to whether a sale is income to you. My guess is that it is.

Further Caution:

Compliance is voluntary. If loaning 10%_again, the magic phrase is "non-repayable loan" – is a hardship, you may without explanation withhold the 10%.

CHAPTER 6: Joint Conclusion to Abortion and the Outlaw and BUCKING POWER

I.

I would propose the following rule be adopted by the Supreme Court: If it comes to light that a decision of the Court is presumed to be erroneous, The Supreme Court, in its original jurisdiction, is the appropriate forum for review. Lower courts are governed by precedent. They have no history of criticizing the Supreme Court. Were I still an active judge, I would be breaking new ground as a lowly trial judge severely taking the Court to task. Thus, *Sebelius* and *Wade – Casey* should be examined by the Court posthaste.

While I may disagree with the results of other Supreme Court decisions, none fall in the category of crying out for immediate reconsideration.

II.

A. This book fits within the spirit of Judge Cardozo's writings in *Growth of the Law*. So, too, *BUCKING POWER: Bad Law and New Order* SVU (?). The latter is a hodge-podge, raising important issues on matters large and small and offering solutions. It opens up a new debate on all sorts of issues. They are legitimate issues, in particular, common societal problems. If the courts reach results contrary to my prejudices (the little guy *BUCKING POWER*), just as long as they are consistent with principle and not merely resting on a history or the judge's bias, which has existed for a long period of time. I as no longer Judge but citizen judging will be placated.

> *Sebelius* is suspect because there are minefields of issues of constitutional magnitude, only some of which I have raised. If the Commerce Clause is put in its proper place, I believe the formulation to be very fragile.

B. With respect to the former, I believe that the basic dispute has been joined on principle. The entire Court in *Casey*, except for Justice Blackmun, who was corrupt for dwelling on *potential life* when he read *Dorland's* definition of embryo as "human organism," obviously, he deceived the Court but didn't mention it. The intentional deception carried over to *Casey* and today.

In light of what has been stated in *Abortion and the Outlaw* in its entirety, the pro-life community can applaud themselves for holding to the ground that the unborn was a human being and a person. Their legal counsel let them down by not looking in office dictionaries, not looking at *Dorland's Illustrated Medical Dictionary*. Finally, the Court noted that the American Medical Association in the 19th Century unanimously agreed that the unborn was a human life from conception; human life is not potential life.

When the AMA voted to approve liberal abortion in the early 1970s, they failed to address the 19th Century conclusion. Thus, as far as I am concerned, it is still the position of the American Medical Association.

Pro-lifers and the government were once again negligent in not making this distinction in *Casey*.

So, I can't place blame on the pro-life constituency for the *Wade* and *Casey* ruling today.

But, the pro-lifers can be blamed for not carefully reading the Bible. True, there are several references to a God's recognition of the unborn in the womb (the citations for which escape me now), but Job 3 is a lightning rod. Death is better than birth; stillborn is better than death. This is because when there is death, there is *no longer suffering*. If the unborn is aborted he does not suffer; if it occurs after he gains sensation, the suffering occasioned by abortion is minimal compared to being born and living for a time.

As I interpret Matthew 7:24-27, the unborn gets an automatic ticket to heaven.

In this light, I find a woman's choice to abort is virtually unlimited. I frown on late term abortions because they do constitute severe *pain and suffering*.

Murder, she wrote. Murder, the right-to-lifers say. Again, returning to the book of Job, God allowed Satan to do anything he wanted to do to Job short of taking his life. From this I take it, NO ONE DIES UNLESS GOD ALLOWS FOR IT.

I believe that God was all-knowing, all-wise and all-powerful as demonstrated at the time Job lived (Possibly Job is just a fable, but if he were a real man, in my estimation, he is the outstanding figure of the *Old Testament*, a precursor of the suffering Jesus).

If this were true at the time Job lived or was written about, it remains true today that God had the power and knowledge and wisdom to stop all abortions were he so inclined.

So, my closing plea is that none dare call abortion murder, but merely killing.

Of course, if my religious views are cast aside on this subject, a closer examination of my 29 or 30 major errors in *Roe v. Wade* must be seriously addressed. As a former, usually successful, judge, I think my statement that the unborn is a person must be recognized by courts because definitions in the dictionary are binding. This is settled law that was insinuated in both *Wade* and *Casey*.

Whether my choice of Bible principles rule the day or the dictionary rules the day, I will be non-critical. But if the court refuses to take up the matter, I will bitch and moan profusely.

And if the issues are resolved on principle, the numerous rallies and protests will cease. My prediction is that the Planned Parenthood Federation and the pro-life community will live in heavenly peace soon.

Suicide and Assisted Suicide

I.

Suicide has traditionally been frowned upon in England and the United States.

> Although acts of suicide are documented through the recorded history of England and this nation, we find no indication of widespread societal approval. To the contrary, suicide was a criminal offense, with significant stigmatizing consequences. As a policy matter, and for practical reasons, suicide was not criminalized in most states (LaFave & Scott, Substantive Criminal Law, § 7.8, pp. 246-251). Lawmakers recognized the futility of punishment and the harshness of property forfeiture and other consequences (*People v. Kevorkian*, 527 N.W. 2d 714, 750-31 (1994)).

Footnote 49 reads as follows:

> At common law, suicide sometimes was referred to as "self murder." Consequences included the forfeiture of property and an ignominious burial (Tsarouhas, n. 36 *supra* at 795, citing Glanville, *The Sanctity of Life and the Criminal Law.* 261-262 (1957), and 4 Blackstone, *Commentaries on the Laws of England* (Oxford: Clarendon Press, 1769), pp. 189, 190, *Kevorkian, supra* 31).

Also, it was assumed that one who committed suicide was suffering from a mental frailty of one sort or another, and thus lacked the necessary mens rea to commit a crime. (Marzen, O'Dowd, Crone & Balch, *Suicide: A constitutional right?* 24 Duquesne L.R. 1, 63, 69, 85-86, 88-89 (1985), *Kevorkian, supra).*

One who assisted a suicide was accorded no such concession, however. At the time the Fourteenth Amendment was ratified, at least twenty-one of the thirty-seven existing states (including eighteen of the thirty ratifying states) prescribed assisted suicide either by statute or as a common-law offense (*Id.* at 76, *Kevorkian, supra).*

Some states have laws criminalizing assisted suicide and all states have involuntary statue commitments for those who may harm themselves.

Approximately a decade after *Kevorkin* was decided, the U.S. supreme court reached the same conclusion. *Washington* v. *Glucksberg,* 521 U.S. 702 (1997) and *Vacco v. Quill,* 521 U.S. 793 (1997).

The United States Supreme Court was in accord with *Kevorkian.* It's study of history was similar to that of Michigan's highest court.

Chief Justice Rehnquist in the lead opinion elicited its conclusion at the outset.

There was no constitutional right to assisted suicide by a physician.

The Court then discussed *Planned Parenthood v. Casey,* 505 U.S. 833 (1992) holding that a state may enact a statute that does not place an undue burden or the right to abort.

The Court concluded:

Throughout the Nation, Americans are engaged in an earnest and profound debate about the morality, legally, and practicality of physician-assisted suicide. Our holding permits this debate to continue, as it should in a democratic society. The decision, in bank the Court of Appeals, is reversed, and the case is remanded for further proceedings consistent with this opinion. *Id.* 753

For my purposes, I want to know who specifically is doing the debating, and on what grounds. Seemingly, the Court was willing to side with one or the other, if only "unnamed experts" could agree and if the popular opinion was in accord.

The Court considered equal protection principles regarding the practice of patients refusing medicine to save life intentionally in *Vacco v. Quill,* 521 U.S. 793 (1997), a companion case.

And concluded:

> For purposes of equal protection challenge to constitutionality of New York's assisted-suicide ban, distinction between assisting suicide and withdrawing life-sustaining treatment, which was permitted by New York law, was rational distinction which comported with fundamental legal principles of causation and intent, even though line between refusing lifesaving medical treatment and assisted suicide may in some cases have been unclear. U.S.C.A. Const. Amend. 14; N.Y.McKinney's Penal Law §§ 120.30, 125-15, subd. 3. 521 U.S. 793

> Under constitutional equal protection analysis, just as state may prohibit assisting suicide while permitting patients to refuse unwanted lifesaving treatment, state may permit palliative care related to that refusal, which may have foreseen but unintended "double effect" of hasting patient's death. U.S.C.A. Const. Amend. 14; N.Y.McKinney's Penal Law §§ 120.30, 125.15, subd. 3. 521 U.S. 793

II.

It seems clear from these cases that atheists, theologians, physicians, and others took up the issue and reached their consensus conclusions.

As far as I can tell, no one specifically addressed the book of Job, perhaps the greatest sufferer in the world, because an innocent man who had never sinned, suffered imminently. He wanted God to end it all – he wanted God to take his life. Job wasn't dying, so suicide is available any time. When one concludes, he is no longer able to pursue happiness, he may end his life.

Apparently, suicide didn't exist at that time – at least the means for committing it: no guns, no knives. I assume no poison, but if there had been poison available, it would have been a slow, painful, more suffering death.

Job was engaged in a series of debates with his three friends who ascertained that he suffered because he was a sinner.

So, Job was asking to plead his case with God to prove that he didn't deserve to suffer. In my view, the high point of Job's discourse over, "What use is life to me, when doomed to death certain?" Job 6:11. Job didn't think his life would ever improve, so God explain to me why I suffer and /or give me relief by ending my life.

The three friends repeatedly emphasized that he suffered because he was a sinner.

God finally did show up.

A. In Chapter 38, God said Job didn't have the wisdom of God. I will quote only the opening lines:

> Then the LORD answered Job out of the whirlwind, and said,
>> "Who *is* this that darkeneth counsel by words without knowledge?
> Gird up now thy loins like a man; for I will demand of thee, and answer thou me.
>> "Where was thou when I laid the foundations of the earth? declare, if thou hast understanding."
> Who hath laid the measures thereof, if thou knowest? or who hath stretched the line upon it?
>> Whereupon are the foundations thereof fastened? or who laid the corner stone thereof;
> When the morning stars sang together, and all the sons of God shouted for joy?
>> Or *who* shut up the sea with doors when it brake forth, as *if* it had issued out of the womb?
> When I made the cloud the garment thereof, and thick darkness a swaddling band for it,

And brake up for it my decreed *place*, and set bars and doors,
And said, Hitherto shalt thou come, but no further: and here
shall thy proud waves be stayed?

Hast thou commanded the morning since thy days: *and*
caused the dayspring to know his place;

That *it* might take hold of the ends of the earth, that the wicked
might be shaken out of it?

It is turned as clay *to* the soul; and they stand as a garment.
Job 38:1-14, King James Bible

The reader is urged to read the rest of Chapter 38.

B. In Chapter 39, God states that he is master of the forces of evil.

Knowest thou the time when the wild goats of the rock bring
forth? *or* canst thou mark when the hinds do calve?

Canst thou number the months *that* they fulfil? or knowest
thou the time when they bring forth?

They bow themselves, they bring forth their young ones, they
cast out their sorrows.

Their young ones are in good liking, they grow up with corn;
they go forth, and return not unto them.

Who hast sent out the wild ass free? or who hath loosed the
bands of the wild ass?

Whose house I have made the wilderness, and the barren
land his dwellings.

He scorneth the multitude of the city, neither regardeth he the
crying of the driver.

The range of the mountains *is* his pasture, and he searcheth
after every green thing.

Will the unicorn be willing to serve thee, or abide by thy crib?

Canst thou bind the unicorn *with* his band in the furrow? or
will he harrow the valleys after thee?

Wilt thou trust him, because his strength *is* great? or wilt thou
leave they labour to him?

Wilt thou believe him, that he will bring home they seed,
and gather *it into* thy barn?

Gavest thou the goodly wings unto the peacocks? or wings and feathers *unto* the ostrich?

Which leaveth her eggs in the earth, and warmeth them in dust. Job 39:1-14, King James Bible

God continues, with the power of Behemoth, more powerful than an ox. He fears nothing. Job 15:25. And, discussed at length leviathan in the sea. All at 25-32, Chapter 41:1-26. God concludes:

Canst thou draw out leviathan with a hook? or his tongue with a cord *which* thou lettest down?

Canst thou put a hook into his nose? or bore his jaw through with a thorn?

Will he make many supplications unto thee? will he speak soft *words* unto thee?

Will he make a covenant with thee? wilt thou take him for a servant for ever?

Wilt thou play with him as *with* a bird? or wilt thou bind him for they maidens?

Shall the companions make a banquet of him? Shall they part him among the merchants?

Canst thou fill his skin with barbed irons? or his head with fish spears?

Lay thine hand upon him, remember the battle, do no more. Behold, the hope of him is in vain; shall *not one* be cast down even at the sight of him?

None *is so* fierce that dare stir him up; who then is able to stand before me?

Who hath prevented me, that I should repay *him? whatsoever is* under the whole heaven *is* mine.

"I will not conceal his parts, nor *his* power, nor his comely proportion.

Who can discover the face of his garment? *or* who can come *to him* with his double bridle?

Who can open the doors of his face? his teeth *are* terrible round about.

His scales *are his* pride, shut up *together as with* a close seal.

One is so near to another, that no air can come between them.

They are joined one to another, they stick together, that they cannot be sundered.

> *By* his blessings a light doth shine, and his eyes *are* like the eyelids of the morning.

Out of his mouth go burning lamps, *and* sparks of fire leap out.

Out of his nostrils goeth smoke, as *out of* a seething pot or caldron.

His breath kindleth coals, and a flame goeth out of his mouth.

In his neck remaineth strength, and sorrow is turned into joy before him.

The flakes of his flesh are joined together: they are firm in themselves; they cannot be moved.

> His heart is as firm as a stone; yea, as hard as a piece of the nether *millstone*.

When he raiseth up *himself*, the mighty are afraid; by reason of breakings they purify themselves.

> The sword of him that layeth at him cannot hold: the spear, the dart, nor the habergeon. King James Bible

Job's response is contained in Chapter 42:

Then Job answered the LORD, and said,

> I know that thou canst do every *thing*, and *that* no thought can be withholden from thee.

Who is he that hideth counsel without knowledge? therefore, have I uttered that I understood not; *things* too wonderful for me, which I knew not.

> Hear, I beseech thee, and I will speak; I will demand of thee, and declare thou unto me.

I have heard of thee by the hearing of the ear; but now mine eye seeth thee.

> Wherefore I abhor *myself*, and I repent in dust and ashes. Job 42:1-6, King James Bible

In the Epilogue, God praises Job for speaking the truth about him and condemning the three friends for not speaking the truth:

And it was *so*, that after the LORD had spoken these words
unto Job, the LORD said to Eliphaz the Temanite, My wrath is
kindled against thee, and against thy two friends: for ye have not
spoken of me *the thing that is* right, as my servant Job *hath*.

Therefore take unto you now seven bullocks and seven rams,
and go to my servant Job, and offer up for yourselves a burnt
offering; and my servant Job shall pray for you: for him will
I accept: lest *I* deal with you *after your* folly, in that ye have
not spoken of me *the thing which is* right, like my servant Job.
So Eliphaz the Temanite and Bildad the Shuhite *and* Zophar the
Naamathite went, and did according as the LORD commanded
them: the LORD also accepted Job.

And the LORD turned the captivity of Job, when he prayed
for his friends: also, the LORD gave Job twice as much as he
had before. Job 42:7-10, King James Bible

C. God blessed Job:

> Thou renewest thy witnesses against me, and increaseth thine
> indignation upon me; changes and war *are* against me. Job
> 10:17, King James Bible

As an aside, all that God wants from my religious leader is truth.
In 1987, I founded *The God of Daniel Religion* with the tenet of "truth."
My sister, a nun, Sister Margaret McTaggart, asked me whether it was
Protestant truth or Catholic truth. I think I remarked that neither was
in sync with God, but there were many things to consider. I don't know
whether I made it up or it comes from some other source, I have often
stated, truth is where you find it.

D. The Book of Job stands for the proposition that no one dies unless
God allows for it. While we decry deaths resulting from a D.U.I., it's
usually on instantaneous death, no pain and suffering.

E. Consider the Ten Commandments:

Thou shalt not murder.

That is an ecclesiastic offense. Any murder defendant has a First Amendment right to be judged by an ecclesiastical court at common law.

All or most states have abolished the common law.

I don't know of any state that has an ecclesiastical court system. I would refer to Matthew 22:21, "Render, therefore unto Caesar the things which are Caesar's; and unto God the things that are God's."

Were I defense counsel in any murder case, I would demur challenging the Court's jurisdiction – "the power to act."

Though history may be contrary to what I am suggesting, conviction must be set aside unless it is adjudicated in a proper forum.

Cain killed Abel in cold blood. His punishment was that he was to roam the world. Death was instantaneous, no pain and suffering.

As Justice Holmes famously began his book on the Common Law, that it was based on *experience* rather than logic, casting aside this experience should be on a case-by-case basis. In other words, any party should be able to rely on the experience of the common law unless it can be demonstrated that new conditions call for a modification of the common law rule in that circumstance.

I no longer have research capabilities, but I'm pretty sure murder wasn't considered in Ecclesiastical courts and common law. If so, that was wrong.

F. In matters of moral issues, The Supreme Court always looks to experts, a wide assortment of do-gooders. That segment of the medical establishment that treats the dying is in a much better position to judge whether assisted suicide is warranted than the medical profession as a whole.

They are the only experts. Panels and commissions of outsiders may, as here, result in very poor results.

I would suggest that the Court has been led astray by do-gooders in the realm of exacting. But, if the Bible speaks, like E.F. Hutton, I demand they listen.

III.

As far as I can tell, the Declaration of Independence has never been argued to apply to physician assisted suicide. I would urge that and appropriate reading is that "it is self evident that all men are created equal, and they are endowed by their creator with certain unalienable rights, that among these are life, liberty, [health] and the pursuit of happiness." Health is not my invention, but it can be traced to the esteemed John Locke, *Letter of Toleration* (1698).

> The commonwealth seems to me to be a society of men constituted only for the procuring, preserving, and advancing their own civil interests.
>
> Civil interests I call life, liberty, health and indolency of body; and the possession of outward things, such as money, lands, houses, furniture, and the like. John Locke,

One's life and one's health are thus paramount or fundamental values, which governments are formed to protect. Each of us want good health and are responsible for safeguarding it.

However, if one's health deteriorates to the extent that death is inevitable in a matter of days, weeks, or months and the illness causes excruciating pain and suffering, the Declaration gives the individual the right and power to swiftly end that person's life.

I maintain that while the government has an obligation to protect human life, the individual is the one to decide whether to end it all, or not. Of course, some for religious reasons or otherwise, will want to tough it out to the bitter end. When one has lost all hope of perusing happiness because of debilitating health it is cruel and inhumane for the state to impose this will in a situation where society has nothing to gain by prolonging life.

To the best of my knowledge, most physicians who deal with end-of-life matters are in favor of assisted suicide, other physicians are opposed. The Supreme Court, as noted above, is swayed in part by the fact that "unnamed experts" cannot reach a consensus. Many in pro-life communities staunchly oppose assisted suicide, the fear of many is that is that it will lead to euthanasia, the involuntary ending of life.

IV.

The Supreme Court ruled that it was constitutional for states to allow physician assisted suicide. Legislatures in five states have given approval (Oregon, Washington, Vermont, Colorado, and California), Montana has done so by court ruling.

The states with legislation has a residency requirement, the individual must be at least 18 years old with life expectancy six months or less, is required that the individual make two oral requests 15 days apart and a written request, each state has differing requirements.

The Montana Supreme Court states "we find no indication in Montana law that physician aid in dying provided to medically competent adult patients is against public policy. Consequently, a physician assisted with the patient's consent is shielded from criminal liability." *Robert Baxter v. Montana (December 31, 2009)*

From my point of view, suicide and assisted suicide are fundamental rights (religion_the book of Job) in life, health, and pursuit of happiness. As such, I wouldn't fiddle-faddle in legislature where strong emotions rule the day. I liked the approach of Montana. However, that ruling may be of limited effect as suicide was not illegal at that state. The homicide statute forbids only the killing of another.

But I would go forward: "it's my life and I'll do as I please."

Were I dying and in pain, suffering, and not in the six states mentioned above I wouldn't wait for the legislature to get off of dead center, I would seize the opportunity in court. I believe I have explained why the two 1997 decisions of the Supreme Court will no longer stand scrutiny.

V.

Job of course wanted God to take his life, because he was perpetually miserable. When one commits suicide and leaves no accompanying note, the reasons would not be evident. Celebrities who seem to have to have it made sometimes take their lives for unknown reasons. If my memory is clear Del Reeves, the star of the Superman T.V. series in the 50's was believed to have committed suicide. Robin Williams, the highly successful comedian, surprised the world when he took his own life.

The advertisers of some drugs offered for sale indicate that suicide is a possible result. A court case in Madison County Nebraska in 2015 revealed that a 15 year old male and a 9 year old girl began a sexual relationship at BoysTown, that lasted for several years.

The defendant, entered a plea of guilty and was sentenced to prison. The girl turned 18 and committed suicide prior to sentencing. The implication at that time was that the behavior of the defendant was an approximate cause of her self-life-taking. The facts also revealed that BoysTown staff and relatives may have pressured her. In other words, she may have been bullied. I have argued in *BUCKING POWER* to be published in June 2017, that a child who has reached puberty is by definition a sexual adult, and accordingly has the right to act sexually as an adult. The underlying principles, are liberty, equal protection, and the pursuit of happiness.

There's also the bible. The good book makes no distinction between adults and minors. So, that "Christian" pressure may be ill-founded biblically. This is suggested in my book, *THE THIRD TESTAMENT: part 1: The God of Daniel Religion 2016.*

Minors are constitutional persons. *Tinker v Des Moines (1969)* But the courts, speaking in generalities often ruled that children are in need of protection unnecessary for adults. This is especially true for sexuality. While a child may consent, legislatures usually hold that the child lacks the legal capacity to consent.

The suicide in the girl in this case may have been a blessing and not a problem. Were she to continue to live, the severe misery likely never would have abated. The pursuit of happiness is none existent.

My philosophy of life, in recent years, is that I am a biblical constitutionalist. I know that may be shocking to many, the youthful male-female-liaison, were offensive to neither the bible nor the constitution.

VI.

While I term one who is suicidal as not in a position to pursue happiness, laymen would probably state that he was severely depressed.

It is not always clear whether a particular death was a suicide or murder (or even an accident). Emory University reports that each year

34,998 people die by taking one's own life. These statistics can be found on the internet.

Apparently, most suicides are accomplished by gunshots, suffocation, and poisoning.

Emory University has indicated that there are 864,950 attempts at suicide each year. The American Foundation for Suicide Prevention has placed an estimate at 750,000 per year. The Parent Resource Program indicates that suicide is the second leading cause of death for youngsters between 10 and 24, and has reported that there are an average of 5,240 attempts by 7-12 graders each day.

CAPITAL PUNISHMENT

If one read the internet the controversy surrounding capital punishment boils down to this: is it moral or immoral?

Before Nebraska's 2016 popular vote on whether the death penalty should be reinstated, I got several phone calls/all from the Nebraska Catholic Bishop's Conference. There message was that capital punishment was wrong, because it was immoral.

I've self-published *THE THIRD TESTAMENT: The God of Daniel Religion 2016,* and voiced several complaints against the church. In a nutshell, they often were not in sync with Jesus's teachings. With respect to capital punishment, was it immoral 2,000 years ago when Jesus allowed himself to be crucified? If so why didn't he speak up?

It is my opinion that morality doesn't shift with the passage of time. Jesus's paramount concern was with "truth," the word of God. "I am the way and the truth and the life. No one comes to the Father except by me."

The word of God does not change over time. The death penalty is just one example of how the Catholic Church (and perhaps others) get themselves into a religious pickle from which there is no way out.

www.ingramcontent.com/pod-product-compliance
Lightning Source LLC
Chambersburg PA
CBHW020514290526
45786CB00002B/599